This book may be recalled before the above date.

THE SOVIET UNION
IN EAST ASIA

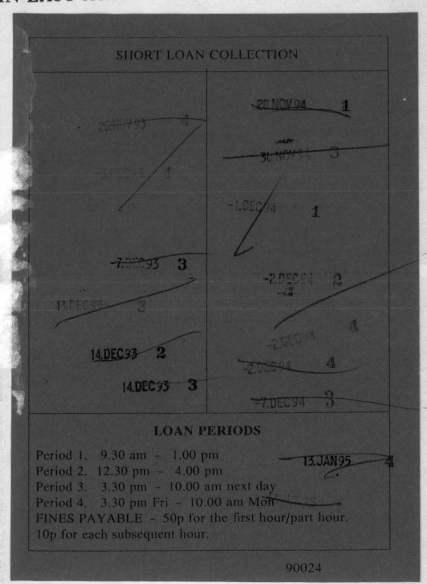

The Royal Institute of International Affairs is an unofficial body which promotes the scientific study of international questions and does not express opinions of its own. The opinions expressed in this publication are the responsibility of the authors.

The Institute and its Research Committee are grateful for the comments and suggestions made by Hugh Seton-Watson and Paul McDonald, who were asked to review the manuscript of this book.

THE SOVIET UNION IN EAST ASIA
Predicaments of Power

edited by
GERALD SEGAL

HEINEMANN
LONDON

WESTVIEW PRESS
BOULDER, COLORADO

Heinemann Educational Books Ltd
22 Bedford Square, London WC1B 3HH

ISBN (U K) 0 435 83777 X
ISBN (U K) 0 435 83778 8 Pbk

Published in the United States of America in 1983 by
Westview Press, Inc.
5500 Central Avenue
Boulder, Colorado 80301

ISBN 0-86531-762-3 (U.S.)

Library of Congress Catalog Card Number: 83-50813

868614
60 00888303

Phototypesetting by Inforum Ltd, Portsmouth
Printed in Great Britain by Biddles Ltd, Guildford, Surrey

Contents

Tables

Editor's Acknowledgements

We are indebted to a number of people and organizations for help in the preparation of this book. The study group meetings in the first half of 1982 were funded by the Social Science Research Council. The Royal Institute of International Affairs provided excellent facilities for these meetings and some members of staff provided especially crucial assistance. In particular, Dr Adeed Dawisha not only ran his usual tight ship so that the study group participants could wander freely on deck, but also took an active and helpful part in most of the discussions on the papers. Miss Ann De'Ath of the RIIA continued to steer the ship through the tricky stages of cajoling contributors into revising drafts, meeting deadlines and calming the often anxious editor. More anonymous debts are of course owed to the participants in the study group who often made trenchant comments, and thanks are also due to the Institute's two readers, Professor Hugh Seton-Waton and Dr Paul McDonald, who spotted errors in the final draft that we all missed first time around.

G.S.

December 1982

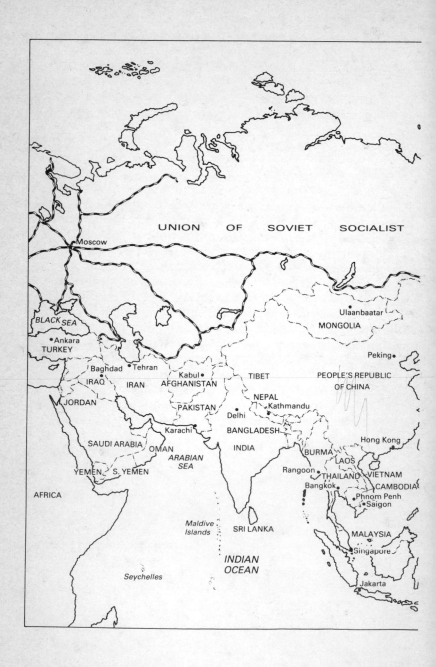

ARCTIC OCEAN

REPUBLICS

CANADA

ALASKA

BERING SEA

Aleutian Islands

Kurile Islands

Vladivostok

NORTH KOREA

SOUTH KOREA

Tokyo

JAPAN

PACIFIC OCEAN

TAIWAN

Manila

PHILIPPINES

NEW GUINEA

INDONESIA

Contributors

David Armstrong, Lecturer, School of International Studies, University of Birmingham

Lawrence Freedman, Professor of War Studies, King's College, University of London

Christina Holmes, research associate, Royal Institute of International Affairs, London

Kazuyuki Kinbara, staff economist, Keidanren (Federation of Economic Organizations)

Malcolm Mackintosh, consultant on Soviet affairs, International Institute for Strategic Studies, London

Wolf Mendl, Reader, Department of War Studies, King's College, University of London

Gerald Segal, Lecturer, Department of Politics, University of Leicester

1 Introduction
Gerald Segal

The Soviet Union is not an east Asian power, but it is a power in east Asia. Other than its European frontiers, no other territory is as vital to Soviet interests as the vast border with east Asia. Thus the essential enduring dilemma of Soviet east Asian policy is set: how to develop a constructive foreign policy in an area where the Soviet Union is over-whelmingly viewed in a hostile light.

This Soviet predicament of power has no simple solution. Three major and very different powers confront the Soviet Union in the area, each of which demands different responses from Moscow. Chinese power, the predominant problem in east Asia, must be met with vigour, but not so much that Beijing is driven to extreme hostility. US power is regional, but more importantly it is also part of a global competition with the Soviet Union. Japanese power is overwhelmingly economic and offers opportunities for beneficial ties to the Soviet Union, but also threatens to buy influence elsewhere in the region at Moscow's expense. Thus the Soviet Union must live not only with different powers in east Asia, but also with different dimensions of military, political and economic relations.

While these predicaments of power are in many senses obvious, it is striking how few analyses have been produced of Soviet policy in east Asia. To be sure, there are excellent more detailed studies of specific aspects of Soviet policy in the region, especially concerning Sino–Soviet relations. There is also at least one attempt to study Soviet policy in Asia as a whole, but it concentrates less on the Soviet perspective.[1] Allen Whiting has recently written a most perceptive analysis of Soviet east Asia, but its emphasis is overwhelmingly on Soviet domestic policy.[2] Apart from the official Soviet view and one dated Western analysis,[3] there are no other comprehensive book-length analyses of Soviet–east Asian relations. This is not to say that such a study is not worthwhile, for as some excellent article-length work makes plain, there is a great deal to analyse.[4]

In order to begin to fill this gap, and come to grips with the Soviet Union's predicaments of power, the Royal Institute of International Affairs convened the third in its current series of study groups on Soviet foreign policy. British experts were gathered from journalism, business, government and universities in the first half of 1982 to produce and comment upon papers covering various aspects of Soviet east Asian policy. The results, as amended after the extensive study group discussions, were prepared for publication as a complement to the two previous RIIA books on Soviet foreign policy dilemmas.[5] It is not by accident – as the Soviet Union is fond of saying – that these books are similar. Whether called dilemmas, problems or predicaments, what is clear is that the Soviet Union has no easy foreign policy options. Like any great power, the Soviet Union finds it difficult confidently to pursue a coherent and consistent strategy in a complex and confusing world.

This latest study of Soviet attempts to live with its predicaments is organized into essentially two main sections, one looking at bilateral Soviet relations, and the other assessing key issues in Soviet policy. These main sections are preceded by a chapter in which Malcolm Mackintosh sets the scene for Soviet east Asian policy. His main theme, and one that runs through much of the book, is the failure of the Soviet Union to become well integrated as an Asian power. The essential features of the Soviet Union remain European, even if the major part of Soviet territory is non-European. Mackintosh suggests that this fundamental problem for Soviet policy arises not merely because the Soviet Union has chosen to remain European, but also because the local states of east Asia do not see the Soviet Union as one of their own. Thus Moscow has found it easier to approach east Asia primarily in balance of power terms, trying to make sense of the contradictory pressures from the local powers as well as its fellow superpower, the United States. Mackintosh also makes plain the centrality of China for Soviet strategy in east Asia, and the continuing inability of the Kremlin to evolve a satisfactory policy for controlling hostility in Sino–Soviet affairs.

China, as the primary problem for Soviet strategy, is the first of the bilateral relations studied in the first core section of the book. Christina Holmes suggests there are no simple solutions to Soviet dilemmas. Sino–Soviet relations are seen as more naturally hostile than amicable, but the level of that hostility need not remain as high as in recent years. The sources of conflict are deep, rooted in geography, ideology and politics. But as strong as these roots might be, they do not necessarily mean that the Soviet Union has no option but to allow China to sway into alliance with the West. Indeed Christina Holmes makes it plain that there are some possibilities of at least a modicum of détente. She is also careful not to be mesmerized by short-term fluctuations in policy, and asserts that Moscow can find no escape from the dilemmas of Sino–Soviet relations.

Before the Sino–Soviet split began to dominate the Soviet Union's Asian policy, the United States had been Moscow's main bilateral problem. David Armstrong does not suggest that Soviet–American relations in east Asia have now suddenly become cooperative, but he does point out that the United States has slipped from first to second position in Soviet regional preoccupations. Soviet–American conflict in the area has steadily declined in intensity, but there remains a bedrock of basically irreconcilable differences. These superpower disagreements stem not so much from local issues, although there are some important ones, but arise primarily because the two powers see themselves as engaged in a global struggle. Therefore any place in the world where the two superpowers are active will inevitably become bound up in global games played by Moscow and Washington. But Armstrong also makes clear that in east Asia, as compared with any other arena of conflict, the Soviet Union has mostly come to accept the primacy of local powers' policies. While the superpowers may find themselves involved in regional conflict, in east Asia the local powers (China and Japan) are so strong, and the problems so complex, that neither Moscow nor Washington can have much confidence in its ability to manipulate events.

After China, Moscow clearly sees Japan as the next most important local power. Wolf Mendl argues that on the surface many would see Soviet–Japanese relations as being similar to Sino–Soviet relations in their deep-rooted hostility. But Mendl suggests this judgement is superficial and fails to take into account the less hostile Soviet–Japanese history or the different international context. Soviet–Japanese relations are more deeply affected by the US factor and are less concerned with military than economic factors. The Japanese appear more flexible in political relations than the Chinese, and the Soviet Union has a less basic fear of Japan than it has of China. Thus, Mendl argues, the Soviet Union has realistic policy options for an improvement of relations with Japan. That these have so far not been exercised, or have been exercised incorrectly, is not to suggest that they cannot be more successful in the future in improving Soviet–Japanese relations. In many senses, in this bilateral relationship more than any other, the Soviet Union has itself to blame for not achieving some kind of breakthrough in ties with Japan.

The final chapter in this first core section attempts to make sense of Soviet–Korean relations. Gerald Segal argues that the Soviet Union has a near hopeless task in sorting out the confusing pressures of policy in this divided country. While all the major powers are involved in some important way in Korea, they are all unable to control local events. The Soviet Union is no exception. Segal points out that in many respects the

Korean vortex is a microcosm of Soviet predicaments in east Asia as a whole.

The second core of this book attempts to study Soviet policy not through bilateral relations, but by analysing key issues in the Soviet perspective. Lawrence Freedman sets the scene by assessing east Asia in Soviet military strategy. China remains the main concern for Soviet planners, and although the Soviet Union does not see its forces in the area as inferior to those of China, it does see a continuing need to retain roughly the present totals. Therefore any major change, for example back to the 1950s levels of minimal forces, seems unlikely, no matter what kind of deal might be struck on the political level with China. Freedman sees US power in east Asia as less worrying to the Soviet Union, but, especially when viewed in the global balance of power, US bases and forces can hardly be ignored. The rapid growth of the Soviet Pacific fleet has now given Moscow at least minimal confidence in the strategic balance, but not nearly enough overwhelming power that it can rest easy. Indeed, as Freedman points out, the paranoia of defence planners in Moscow is unlikely to be calmed on either the Chinese or US front. And so, while the Soviet Union has no cause for insecurity in strategic terms, neither can the paranoid voices be silenced. The differing potential threats from local powers and the United States will ensure no paucity of problems for the paranoid.

While the military aspect looks gloomy, there is room for greater optimism on economic policy in east Asia. Kazuyuki Kinbara focuses on the Japanese potential for Soviet economic policy. He argues that vast Soviet dreams of Japanese economic aid or investment in east Asia have clearly been dashed and there are profound economic and political reasons for some future pessimism in this respect. But Kinbara points to important areas where more realistic economic deals are possible. For such progress to be made, however, important alterations in both Japanese and Soviet policy are needed. But, as Kinbara points out, Soviet dreams of a huge Japanese economic potential, like Western illusions about the China market, are unlikely to be satisfied.

The problems and predicaments in Soviet policy in east Asia are summed up by Gerald Segal in the conclusion. In a wide-ranging survey of Soviet policy few optimistic aspects for Soviet planners appear. Certain specific elements, for example Soviet–Japanese economic relations, are seen as offering some hope for future change. But overall the Soviet Union is found to be reconciled to the complexity of east Asia and to its own inability to manipulate events. If there is any certainty in Soviet policy, it is the certainty of uncertainty.

Finally, something must be said about the scope and the purposes of this book. The main theme concerns the predicaments of Soviet power in east Asia. It is assumed that these predicaments have changed with time, but that there is no escape for the Soviet Union from the enduring complexities of east Asian international relations. Precisely because of these complexities, it is impossible to find a single over-arching explanation of Soviet policy. No attempt is therefore made to offer pithy generalizations. Neither are far-reaching predictions of Soviet policy suggested. The authors attempt to reduce the basic dimensions of Soviet policy to their simplest components, but do not attempt more. It should also be noted that the scope of the book is limited to east Asia not including south-east Asia. The special problems of south-east Asia will be tackled in a future RIIA study, since the issues were felt to be distinct and important enough to warrant individual treatment.

Notes
[1] Bhabani Sen Gupta, *Soviet–Asian Relations in the 1970's* (New York, Praeger, 1976).
[2] Allen Whiting, *Siberian Development and East Asia* (Stanford, Calif., Stanford University Press, 1981).
[3] Ivan Kovalenko, *Soviet Policy for Asian Peace and Security* (Moscow, Progress Publishers, 1979); and Geoffrey Jukes, *The Soviet Union in Asia* (Berkeley, Calif., University of California Press, 1973).
[4] Donald Zagoria, 'The Soviet quandary in Asia', *Foreign Affairs*, January 1978; Harold Hinton, 'East Asia', in Kurt London (ed.), *The Soviet Union in World Politics* (Boulder, Colo., Westview Press, 1980); and Thomas Robinson, 'The Soviet Union and Asia in 1981', *Asian Survey*, vol. 22, no. 1 (January 1982).
[5] Karen Dawisha and Philip Hanson (eds), *Soviet–European Dilemmas* (London, Heinemann for the RIIA, 1981); and Adeed Dawisha and Karen Dawisha (eds), *The Soviet Union in the Middle East* (London, Heinemann for the RIIA, 1982).

2　Soviet Attitudes towards East Asia
Malcolm Mackintosh

The attitudes of the Soviet Union to the countries of the Far East, in particular China and Japan, have been based on a number of fundamental geographical, historical and political factors which have formed Russian and then Soviet thinking about an area of the world in which the Soviets believe that they have important and justifiable interests. This chapter begins with an attempt to examine these basic factors and then discusses the main issues involved for the Soviet Union: the Sino–Soviet dispute, the Soviet relationship with Japan and the role of the United States in the area. The chapter concludes with a brief look at how the Soviets might see the development of their main interests in the present phase and the foreseeable future.

Background factors

The Soviet Union's claims to be an Asian power and thus to play a major role in the Far Eastern region is founded on the geographical fact that Soviet territory extends in one unbroken landmass from Europe across the northern hemisphere into Asia. The Soviet Pacific coastline is close to Japan and Korea, and large stretches of Soviet Siberia border on China and Mongolia – all genuinely indigenous Asian powers with Asian civilizations and histories. The geographical presence of the Soviet Union in Asia, however, does not make the Russians an Asian people – in the sense that Russian civilization, culture and patterns of behaviour in external relations cannot easily be linked to the traditions of the peoples and nations of Asia as they have developed in the Asian physical and human environment.

It is beyond the scope of this chapter to define the essential elements of Asian attitudes to internal, foreign or defence policies which may differ from those of 'European' or 'imperial-European' traditions, especially concerning social, religious or diplomatic factors. There are, however, certain practices, which can be identified with the historical expansion of the power of European states. For example, Western forms of political evolution and the search for economic resources overseas were achieved by using a distinctive pattern of military and especially naval power. Broadly speaking, these patterns were not indigenous to Asian tradition but some have been borrowed or followed by Asian states as they developed contacts with European powers in the past few hundred years. The Soviet Union has proved to be a determined supporter of these attitudes and policies.

But to return to the practical evidence that the Soviet far east is an extension of European Russia into Asia: Soviet cities in Siberia, such as Vladivostok, Khabarovsk or Irkutsk, are Russian and European cities, built by Europeans for Europeans. The great majority of the people in thinly populated Siberia are Russians, and the governmental structure of Siberia places it within the Russian Soviet Federated Socialist Republic (RSFSR), whose headquarters is in Moscow, under a purely European leadership. The elements of Soviet power in the Soviet Union's far east are also in European hands: particularly the Communist Party organizations and the armed forces. The Pacific fleet, the high command of Soviet forces in the far east, now under Army General Govorov, and its subordinate military districts, and the frontier-guard troops of the KGB are almost all commanded by Russians or Ukrainians. Moreover, the economy and heavy industry of Siberia and its centres of science and technology are largely controlled by men and women of European origin.

To the south of Siberia lie a number of non-European, non-Russian republics whose importance is not only growing but whose longer-term impact on the nature of the Soviet Union is well recognized in Moscow. The population of republics such as Kazakhstan, Uzbekistan and Tadzhikistan will, by the end of the century, provide a high proportion of adult Soviet citizens. Soviet leaders realize that the influence of non-European nationalities will have to be taken fully into account as their percentage of the Soviet population grows. For example in April 1982 Brezhnev chose Tashkent in Central Asia as the location for a major speech on Asian affairs.

Nevertheless, the traditional Soviet and Russian way of coping with this problem has been to continue to concentrate state and political power in these republics in European hands: the tradition dies hard in the Soviet Union. Key posts in the Republic's Party organizations – such as the second Party secretary whose responsibilities include personnel matters, appointments and liaison with the armed forces and the KGB – are normally held by Russians. Genuine Uzbeks, Tadzhiks or Kazakhs play little part in the realities of Soviet power and so far have not contributed in any significant way to introducing Asian ideas in the formulation of Soviet foreign, military or economic policies in Asia, in political thought or in planning the development of Soviet relations with Asian states.

The first point to be made, therefore, is that whatever role the Soviet Union seeks to play in Asia, and whatever aims and interests it may have there, they belong to a European and a global power in Asia and not to an Asian power acting on Asian political and social assumptions and using Asian negotiating techniques. Indeed, this can be traced back to Russia's historical role in northern Asia: its advance to the Pacific in the seventeenth and eighteenth centuries, absorbing large areas of the Old Chinese empire as it went; its clash with Japan in 1904 and again in 1945; and its territorial acquisitions at the end of the Second World War. The whole attitude of mind, therefore, underlying Soviet decisions in this area is that of a strongly nationalist, European power with a long tradition of expansion eastwards, now reinforced by a sense of political mission based on an ideology: that of Marxism–Leninism.

The next major factor in the Soviet attitude to Asia is the status of the Soviet Union as a superpower. The country's superpower status is based on its size, its growing population (now 265 million) and its developing economic and technological achievements. But the factor which really convinced the Soviet leadership in the late 1960s that they had achieved this status was the military one: the Soviet Union's strategic nuclear armoury and its emergence at sea as a global naval power. In the eyes of the Soviet leaders, superpower status confers on the Soviet Union rights of involvement in the affairs of important parts of the world, including Asia. It is up to the Soviet leadership, as the Russians see it, to decide where, when and at what level the Soviet Union should become involved in any particular situation.

There are, of course, many forms which Soviet involvement could take. What is essential in the Soviet view is that all countries in Asia or those which are geographically outside Asia but have interests in the region should neither question nor challenge the *right* of the Soviet Union to pursue Asian policies of its own choice. The means to be employed could be diplomatic, political, economic or military; or a combination of all four, with the added dimension of subversion where this may be appropriate.

Finally, in this brief look at the background factors, mention should be made of the Soviet Union's economic interests in relation to its territories in Asia. Two-thirds of Soviet territory lies to the east of the Ural mountains and contains a high proportion of the Soviet Union's actual and potential wealth in energy resources, minerals, precious metals and timber. Siberia is still to a large extent regarded in Moscow as an underdeveloped territory (in spite of the construction of the Baikal–Amur (BAM) railway) and the Soviet Union would like to speed up its exploitation with the help of foreign credits and technology.

Although other events in Soviet policy, such as the invasion of Afghanistan in 1979, have placed restrictions on the willingness of a number of advanced countries to provide this aid, the search for foreign help in exploiting Siberian resources plays a part among the factors on which Soviet Asian policy is based.

These major factors, political, military and economic, form the basis of Soviet thinking and policy formulation on Far Eastern affairs in the present phase. They indicate the way in which Asia and its problems and potential opportunities for Soviet policies are considered and analysed in Moscow, and in a sense they form starting points from which these policies are then planned and undertaken. They do not, in practice, indicate necessarily what priority is going to be assigned by the Soviet government to a particular issue – for example, the importance to be given to the economic or strategic factors in an area of crisis or opportunity – and they cannot tell us in what direction Soviet policies will go with any degree of certainty.

Soviet aims and priorities in Asia
Throughout the period under review Soviet attitudes, aims and priorities in Asia have concentrated on the Soviet relationships with China, Japan and the United States, with secondary interests in Korea and south-east Asia, including Vietnam, Kampuchea and Laos. There can be no doubt that at present the Soviet attitude to China and the Chinese comes first in these priorities, though this was not always so. In the pre-war years Japan, as the greatest military power in Asia, occupied this position; and some of the European empires, including the British, the French and the Dutch, were regarded by the Soviet Union as influential in some fields, including trade and commerce. The main change came, in all probability, with the assumption of real power by the Chinese Communist Party in 1949. The United States probably came to occupy its prominent position in Asia, in Soviet thinking, since the end of the Second World War in 1945 – a position greatly reinforced by the US role in that war in Asia and the success of UN forces under US commands in the Korean War of 1950–3.

The Soviet attitude to China
It is probably true to say that even today the Soviet attitude to China still includes elements of historical and traditional Russian views of China. It is based on an inherited fear of China's size and numbers, the ethnic factor described in Russian literature as the 'Yellow Peril', and, at the same time, a certain contempt for China's economic backwardness. Most early contacts of Russians with Chinese took place during the long decline of the Chinese empire. Certainly this element of fear remains in Soviet attitudes to China today; but so does a sense of

'superiority' which, especially when expressed in economic, industrial or military terms, has given the typical Soviet a feeling of confidence that in the event of conflict between the two powers China could not expect to win.

The development of communism in China from the 1920s to the 1940s, leading to the overthrow of the US-supported Nationalist regime in 1949, added a new dimension to the Sino–Soviet relationship. The Soviets welcomed the conquest of Asia's largest country by a communist party which seemed loyal and obedient to the Soviet Union: Mao Zedong appeared to have a great admiration for Stalin. They also encouraged the use of China's military power to support Soviet and 'world communist' causes, such as the involvement of the Chinese Red Army in the Korean War in 1950. At the same time the Soviet Party leaders, expressing the instinctive convictions of the Russian people, felt that the Chinese ought to recognize the innate political, ideological, economic and industrial superiority of the Soviet Union, accept political guidance and orders from Moscow without question, agree to Soviet demands and concepts of military collaboration and economic aid, and echo all Soviet pronouncements on foreign affairs. Communist China should act as a large and populous Asian 'satellite' of the Soviet Union similar to those of the Soviet bloc in Eastern Europe.

While Stalin was alive Mao Zedong broadly speaking accepted this role, recognizing the devastation in China caused by two decades of war and China's destitute economic condition. But after 1955 China began to resent the 'superiority' displayed by the Soviet Union. Chinese leaders felt that as their country recovered from the civil war it ought to be treated by the Soviet Union as an ideological and political ally rather than a satellite. Mao and his colleagues believed that China had a right to initiate policies at home and abroad – for example, the offshore islands crisis in 1958 and the Great Leap Forward in 1959. China also expected Soviet assistance in building a Chinese nuclear capability for the People's Liberation Army – a prospect which horrified not only Khrushchev but also the Soviet military leaders of that time.

By 1960, for these and other reasons, some of them of an ideological nature, China and the Soviet Union entered a period of dispute which eventually covered all aspects of their relationship: Party to Party, state to state, military, commercial and economic. The development of this dispute and events in China since the death of Mao are beyond the scope of this chapter, and are discussed in the following one. For our purposes here, the most interesting aspect of the dispute is probably the almost instinctively traditionalist or, as the Chinese would say, 'neocolonialist hegemonistic' element of the Soviet handling of the crisis. The Soviet Union's first reaction when the dispute appeared was to recall at the shortest possible notice all its military and civilian advisers in China – to the detriment of China's economic, industrial and military power. The Soviet Union then began to build up its military forces from 12 divisions in 1963 to around 47 in 1982, together with significant increases in air, naval and missile power: the first SS–20s to be deployed in the Soviet Union were against China. Soviet troops were deployed into Mongolia in 1967; frontier clashes occurred between Soviet and Chinese frontier guards in the 1960s, of which those in 1969 were the worst; and by 1980 the Soviet armed forces had set up a supreme high command (STAVKA) for all its forces in the Far East, but primarily to deal with China.

Politically and diplomatically the Soviet Union tried in traditional ways to isolate China and to trap it in the limited negotiations, for example on border issues, in which the two countries were engaged. The Soviets also sought to undermine China's activity in the Third World and rally as much support as they could within the communist bloc for anti-Chinese policies and statements. These policies, especially the military build-up, were characteristically Soviet concepts, and demonstrated the way in which the Soviet Union instinctively reacts when dealing with opposition within the communist world.

We cannot predict the next stage in Soviet policy-making towards China. Certainly the Soviets would like to see a Chinese leadership in power which replaced its opposition to the Soviet Union by a cooperative and, in the last resort, an obedient attitude to Moscow's wishes and demands. The Soviets are particularly anxious to increase their knowledge of events and personalities in China to see if there are any potentially pro-Soviet figures in the Party or the armed forces. But in a purely speculative view it would be characteristic of the Soviet Union to explore the possibilities of ultimately encouraging by political, ideological or subversive means the loosening of central control in China and increasing the chance that tomorrow's China might be 'regionalized' – as has happened before in Chinese history, when warlords ruled parts of the country as regional dictators.

Of course the Soviets realize that throughout most of China's years of power and influence the central authority of the state was paramount. But some Soviet leaders might consider the potential advantages to the Soviet Union of being able to try, at best, to 'play off' one regional ruler against another, and thus perhaps increase Soviet influence in that vast country. On the other hand, such an approach would be second best to controlling a central government with the right ideological convictions and sense of obedience to Moscow. Other, rival powers might also seek to exploit regionalism in China, and this could lead to additional confrontations, for example with the United States, in the area, and there is the added problem that one or more of these regions might fall under Muslim influence in religion or politics. The preferred Soviet option, therefore, would be to work to dominate the central government and Party leadership in the China of the future.

The Soviet attitude to Japan

Historically the Russian attitude to Japan began with a picture of mid-nineteenth-century Japan as an underdeveloped and feudal Asian state which was unlikely to offer any serious resistance to Russian imperial expansion in the East. The Russians did, however, observe the rapid advance of Japan at the end of the century to modernization in the economic, administrative and military fields. They learnt something of Japan's existing and potential power from the defeat the Russian army and navy suffered from the Japanese in the war of 1904–5, which was, incidentally, fought mainly on Chinese territory as both the Russian and the Japanese empires pushed further into China.

The long-drawn-out Japanese invasion of China from 1931 to 1945 involved Soviet aid to both the communists and the Nationalists in China and also Soviet–Japanese military clashes on the border, for example those in 1938 and 1939. In August 1945, after the end of the Second World War in Europe, the Soviet Union entered the war against Japan and, in a rapid three-week campaign in Manchuria, defeated the Guandong army and recovered all the Far Eastern territories Russia had lost in 1905.

Since the end of the Second World War in the Far East, the Soviet Union has tried to develop and increase Soviet influence in Japanese political life and to detach Japan from its alliance with the United States. It has also tried to exploit Japanese financial and technological resources and skills in the interests of the economic development of Siberia. In diplomatic relations the Soviets have demonstrated their commitment to the 'imperial' concept of retaining all territories acquired either by Russia before the Revolution or by the Soviet Union during the Second World War. In spite of the potential advantages to the USSR of some flexibility on this issue, for example over the southern Kurile islands, no Soviet leader has seriously offered even to discuss the problem with the Japanese.

In trying to assess the Soviet attitude to Japan we must stress Moscow's respect for and recognition of Japan's economic and political successes, its wealth and prestige, especially in the international business community, and the capacity for hard work and discipline of the Japanese people. The Soviets are in fact torn between what they regard as their nationalist and ideological rights, their strategic advantages and the 'fruits of victory' in 1945, on the one hand, and their recognition of the breakthrough which might occur in Soviet–Japanese political relations if they made the concessions on the territorial issues sought by Japan, on the other. Such concessions might even weaken

Japan's apparently unending willingness to provide financial and economic aid to China – a factor which worries the Soviet Union very considerably.

It seems unlikely, however, that any predictable Soviet government would be ready to take the risks inherent in the cession of Soviet territory to Japan. Fundamentally the Russians' inherited dislike of Japan continues to dominate much Soviet thinking on that country, and national and strategic issues continue to take priority over even the most promising economic advantage. No doubt the Soviets will try to improve relations and explore ways of appealing to Japanese interests without conceding what the Japanese want – the return of the southern Kurile islands. The Soviets may also hope that in the longer term political trends in Japan might produce a more favourable attitude among young Japanese to Soviet aims and this might promote better relations with the Soviet Union. In the short term, however, Soviet expectation of detaching Japan from the West (and from China) is probably very limited, and the Soviets will assume that a change in the balance of power in the Far East through an improvement in their relationship with Japan is unlikely in the foreseeable future.

The Soviet attitude to the United States in the Far East

There are, of course, many areas of activity in the Far East of interest to the Soviet Union, which are dealt with in other papers. These include, as already mentioned, the Soviet relationship with North Korea. There are also longer-term Soviet economic, political or even military interests in a presence in some of the new island states of the Pacific Ocean. But there can be no doubt that a very high place in Soviet priorities in Asia goes to the role of the United States in the area, and to Soviet attitudes to that role in the present phase.

Basically the Soviet Union realizes that although the United States came later into the Asian field than Russia, it now has a well-established history of influence in the area from Japan to China, south-east Asia and the Pacific. The United States played the major role in winning the war in the Pacific in 1941–5, and in defeating North Korean aggression in 1950. It supported the Nationalists in the external and civil wars in China, and still maintains support for Nationalist Taiwan. The United States also witnessed the defeat of its friends and allies in Vietnam at the hands of pro-Soviet communists in the 1970s – and with much loss of US life and self-confidence in military options. On the other hand, the United States dominates much of the Pacific Ocean in political, military and strategic terms, has a strong and lasting relationship with Commonwealth countries such as Australia, New Zealand and Singapore, and also good relations with the Philippines, Thailand and Indonesia, and has solid defence alliances with Japan and South Korea.

When the Soviet leaders assess the realities of the balance of power in Asia, they must realize that no major Asian issue can be settled without the involvement of the United States.

The central theme of Soviet thinking on the role of the United States in Asia is that it too is basically that of a large Western (if not strictly European) power with 'imperial' pretensions and a dedication to capitalism in social and economic terms and to military power as an important means of preserving an existing presence and in seeking to expand its influence further afield. In this sense the Soviets do not regard the United States as an indigenous Asian power, and they expect the Americans to pursue their policies in Asia in roughly the same way as they do in Europe, the Middle East or elsewhere in the Third World. Indeed, the Soviet Union sees the confrontation with the United States in Asia as one part of the global 'correlation of forces' (to use a favourite Soviet phrase) in which power and the forging of alliances and groupings of states in favour of one side or the other have very important parts to play.

This concept leads on to consideration of one element of the Soviet attitude to the role of the United States in Asia which is also characteristic of the traditional concept of power in Soviet thinking: the existence (as the Soviets see it) of the 'east Asian quadrilateral', consisting of America, China, Japan and the Soviet Union. The Soviets find the classification of international relationships in a particular area as 'groupings' of this kind irresistible. It is not in any identifiable form a Marxist–Leninist concept as understood and practised by the Soviet Union. The Soviets believe that their concept of the quadrilateral is essentially a state-to-state relationship and that it is the United States' aim, since it cannot exclude the Soviet Union from the group, to isolate the Soviet Union and continue to ensure that it remains the odd man out.

The Soviet task, therefore, is to defeat this policy, and secure greater Soviet influence within the quadrilateral. In theory, it could do so. Acting in its capacity as a superpower with a 'special relationship' with the United States on strategic nuclear weapons issues, it might try to make a deal with Washington on strategic matters which by-passed the existing balance in the quadrilateral and, hopefully, moved towards negotiating on Asian issues with the United States outside the grouping. This seems, however, unlikely in the light of the attitude of the present administration in Washington to Soviet strategic weapons superiorities, and of the US attitude to the Soviet invasion of Afghanistan and other problems in East–West relations. But the Soviets will probably go on trying.

Again, in theory, the Soviet Union would like to detach Japan from the US side in the quadrilateral. We have already discussed possible

Soviet ways of influencing Japan to do so, and much is made in Soviet approaches to Japan of alleged attempts by the United States to use some Asian issues to promote or protect US business and trade interests in the area. But the likelihood is that the essential territorial concessions required by Japan will not be made by the Soviet side, and that Japan's interest in changing its alignment in the area is likely to be minimal.

Then there is China. A restoration of a working collaboration with a pro-Soviet communist regime in China would not only be ideologically satisfying to Moscow but would cause a major realignment within the quadrilateral. Certainly the Soviet Union looks with some hope on the apparent worsening of relations between Washington and Beijing over the former's continuing interest in military and economic aid for Taiwan. But, as the Russians see it, this would not of itself be enough to lead to a change in Chinese attitudes to the Soviet Union. And for the reasons mentioned above, there is little likelihood of an ideological or major state-to-state rapprochement between China and the Soviet Union in the predictable future.

In the minds of the leaders in Moscow, the concept of the east Asian quadrilateral in which the Soviet Union is the odd man out is, therefore, likely to remain paramount. The present Soviet leaders cannot foresee an improvement in the balance of power in Asia favourable to Moscow. In making this judgement we realize that it is a speculative one, and some of the factors we have accepted as important and valid may alter or even disappear: perhaps under the influence of a new and younger Soviet leadership in the late 1980s or the 1990s about whose likely policies in Asia we have no reliable evidence.

What is not likely to change, however, is the *nature* of the Soviet attitude to Asia. It will almost certainly continue to be that of a superpower with a 'European' or 'imperial–European' kind of nationalism, combined with the Soviet Union's contemporary form of communist ideology, which is often rather remote from classical Marxism. It is bound to be dependent on the Soviet concept of the role and size of Soviet military power in the area, and the Soviet Union will, for strategic and traditional Russian reasons, interpret the situation in Asia as a series of groupings, spheres of influence leading to a balance of power in Asia in political and military terms. If this turns out to be the case, the possibility that the Soviet Union's role in Asian affairs will change and acquire genuinely Asian characteristics with a real understanding of Asian thinking, Asian standards and Asian associations will, as far as we can see, be rather remote.

3   The Soviet Union and China
Christina Holmes

Analysing Sino–Soviet relations is anything but simple. There has been no dearth of major shifts in bilateral ties since 1949, and these changes have, in many cases, had a fundamental impact on international relations and the strategic balance. In the formulation of Soviet policy in the Far East, no single relationship is as crucial as Moscow's dealings with Beijing.

In 1950 the friendship between the Soviet Union and China seemed to many an unshakable alliance pitting East against West and communism against democracy. Yet in the mid-1950s the communist giants began to drift apart. With border clashes in 1969 providing dramatic evidence of the split one commentator wrote that the two were on a collision course towards war.[1] Sino–Soviet war did not materialize, but neither was the rift healed. The dispute is still of enormous significance today as both China and the Soviet Union are communist states, both are nuclear powers, both are members of the UN Security Council and both command vast tracts of strategically important land rich in natural resources. This split in the communist ranks has been of tremendous strategic significance. It was in part the fear of the Marxist–Maoist monolith that fuelled McCarthyism during the 1950s, and the demise of the monolith provided a catalyst for Sino–American détente in the early 1970s. The secret meetings between Henry Kissinger and top Chinese leaders and the subsequent meeting between President Richard Nixon and Chairman Mao Zedong paved the way for normalization of Sino–American relations. In the meantime, Sino–Soviet competition for influence, particularly in the Third World, led to indirect clashes between the two sides and a proliferation of new alignments.

That Soviet leaders are deeply concerned about their populous neighbour to the south is obvious. Since Mao's death in September 1976 there have been numerous overtures from Moscow aimed at improving relations, the latest of which came when President Leonid Brezhnev, speaking at Baku on 26 September 1982, indicated that normalization of relations with China was the main priority of Soviet policy in Asia. Beijing has been cool to many previous Soviet overtures, but important changes can never be ruled out. The official visit by Soviet Deputy Foreign Minister Ilyichev in October 1982 for 'talks about talks' marks the resumption of bilateral negotiations after China suspended contacts in the wake of the Soviet invasion of Afghanistan. In November the new Andropov-led Soviet regime made it plain that Brezhnev's overtures to China were still important and would be pursued. The importance of the new developments are not to be underestimated. Just as the Sino–Soviet split was in certain respects a windfall for the West, so a Sino–Soviet rapprochement might be equally important in causing a Western reassessment of its security.

Analysing these momentous shifts in a brief chapter must necessarily be limited. By highlighting the major trends before the 1969 watershed, it will be possible to prepare the ground for an assessment of present policy. The result is inevitably impressionistic, but it is hoped that the main dilemmas of Sino–Soviet relations will emerge more clearly.

From cooperation to conflict

Some would say that the roots of the dispute lie far back in the pillage and plunder of the Mongol hordes, in the gradual encroachment of Russian explorers, hunters and trappers, in the 'unequal treaties' forced on the Chinese by the Russian tsars and later in Stalin's decision to aid Nationalist forces in China from 1921 to 1949 instead of the struggling communists. This legacy of hostility cannot be ignored. To focus on the more recent past, however, is not to ignore history but simply to accept that legacy as a given.

Mao Zedong proclaimed the establishment of the People's Republic of China on 1 October 1949, and on 14 February 1950 he and Joseph Stalin signed the Sino–Soviet treaty of friendship, alliance and mutual assistance in Moscow. The Chinese needed Soviet assistance to rebuild their war-torn country and to overcome their economic backwardness. Mao apparently drove a hard bargain and discussions with Stalin were frequently acrimonious.[2] Having defeated the Japanese 'imperialists' and seen the backs of forces which had partitioned China, Mao was determined that China should be treated as an equal on the world stage. Expectations were high, but it was not long before it became clear to Chinese leaders that Soviet economic 'aid' had strings attached and was, in fact, little more than normal trade between the two countries.[3] The disappointed expectations of Chinese leaders were an important source of the friction that developed between the two sides. The Soviet expectation of repayment for war materials supplied to the Chinese 'volunteers' following the Korean War which began in June 1950 is a concrete example of the kind of treatment resented by Chinese leaders.

The personal relationship between Mao and Stalin had steadily deteriorated after the signing of the friendship treaty, and Stalin's death in March 1953 provided the opportunity for an overture on the part of his successor. Khrushchev, first secretary of the Soviet Communist Party (CPSU), travelled to China in 1954 with Deputy Premier and Minister of Defence Nikolai Bulganin. Khrushchev lavished praise on the Chinese and a number of agreements were reached.[4] The joint communiqué signed at the end of the visit stressed that China should occupy an equal place in world affairs. Khrushchev thus recognized and played to Chinese sensitivities and the mid-1950s were comparatively good years in Sino–Soviet relations.

In 1956, however, new sources of tension slowly began to undermine the friendship. At the CPSU Congress on 20 February Khrushchev seemed to extend the concept of 'peaceful coexistence' to relations with developed capitalist states, rejected the concept of the 'inevitability of war' and admitted that 'peaceful transition' to socialism was possible – all ideological anathemas to Chinese leaders. He also made a positive reference to the control of nuclear weapons which worried Beijing since the Chinese were perhaps hoping to receive nuclear technology and possibly a sample bomb from the Soviet Union. In his 'secret' concluding remarks to the Congress Khrushchev denounced Stalin. There had been no advance warning to the delegates or Party leaders and Chinese leaders were later to blame Moscow for having caused 'confusion within the Parties' culminating in the Polish and Hungarian crises in the summer and autumn of 1956. Although the extent of their disagreement was not vast at the time, Chinese leaders later dated the beginning of the Sino–Soviet rift from the 20th Congress and the 'road of revisionism taken by the leadership of the CPSU'.[5]

The Moscow Meeting of Representatives of Communist and Workers' Parties in November 1957 reflected a better atmosphere. The crises in Eastern Europe had convinced Chinese leaders of the need for strong bloc leadership; the first successful test of a Soviet ICBM on 26 August 1957 and the first Sputnik launching on 4 October had led Mao and his colleagues to believe that the socialist camp was now invincible; and a Sino–Soviet agreement 'on new technology for national defence' had been signed on 15 October. It was in the heady confidence of Chinese leaders, as opposed to the more cautious approach of Moscow to world affairs, that the seeds of future conflict lay. US intervention in Lebanon in July 1958, and possibly also the Taiwan straits crisis later that summer, brought home to both sides their divergent views on the means of pursuing international objectives. Chinese leaders scorned Khrushchev's attempts to deal with the Lebanese crisis by diplomatic means alone, and Soviet promises of support for China's claim to Taiwan were less than China expected.[6] Khrushchev's unwillingness to act decisively to further the aims of the international socialist movement brought into question the reliability of the Soviet Union as a military ally and strengthened Beijing's desire for its own nuclear deterrent.[7]

China's domestic policies at the time were also a source of friction with the Soviet Union. In the summer of 1958 Khrushchev was disturbed by Chinese claims to be able to leapfrog stages of economic and social development and thus reach the stage of 'communism' more quickly. Experience of Moscow's niggardliness was leading Mao and other Chinese leaders to try to go it alone. At the Third Congress of the Romanian Workers' Party in Bucharest, held between 20 and 26 June 1960, the CPSU and the Chinese Communist Party (CPC) attacked each other by name. The Chinese protested that Khrushchev had violated the principle of settling questions of common concern 'by consultation among the fraternal parties'.

Natural calamities, coupled with Soviet pressure throughout 1959 and 1960, increased the determination of the Chinese to find their own development path. In August 1960 Khrushchev decided to give them the opportunity to do just that when he announced the withdrawal of Soviet experts from China. At the Moscow Conference of Eighty-One Communist and Workers' Parties in November 1960 only the Albanian delegation gave the CPC any real support. In the summer of 1961, the Soviet Union and some East European countries imposed economic sanctions on Albania while China stepped up its economic aid. Albania thus became a symbol of Sino–Soviet differences, as was Yugoslavia, which was seen by Mao as the symbol of revisionism. Soviet leaders often referred to Albania while the real target of criticism was Beijing. Chinese statements castigated 'Tito revisionism' when the finger was really meant to point at Khrushchev. What is more, China's territorial dispute with India, culminating in the border war of October 1962, provided evidence of the unwillingness of Soviet leaders to support China's 'adventurist schemes'. Soviet neutrality incensed Chinese leaders who accused Moscow of taking the side of a 'capitalist country' led by a 'reactionary elite' against a fraternal socialist state.[8]

The Cuban missile crisis occurred almost simultaneously with the Sino–Indian border conflict, and added fuel to China's complaints about Soviet timidity. Beijing at first announced its support for the Soviet decision to place missiles in Cuba, but when Khrushchev backed down on 27 October Chinese leaders denounced the decision to place missiles in Cuba as 'adventurism' and the decision to take them out as 'capitulationism'.[9] Khrushchev was stung by Chinese criticism and subsequently taunted Mao in a major speech to the Supreme Soviet on 12 December 1962, in which he asked why the Chinese, if they were so brave, had failed to take back Hong Kong and Macao. In their reply of 8

March 1963 Chinese leaders listed the 'unequal treaties' imposed on China by Tsarist Russia, thus for the first time injecting the territorial element into the open Sino–Soviet polemics.[10]

Soviet leaders tried to mend fences at the beginning of 1963, calling for unity of the communist parties and for a joint meeting of representatives of the CPC and the CPSU to set the stage for a conference of Marxist–Leninist parties.[11] The Sino–Soviet meeting opened on 5 July 1963, but was unsuccessful. Beijing was angered by the conclusion later that month of the test-ban treaty, which Chinese leaders saw as a Soviet–US plot to keep China and others out of the nuclear club. Mao saw this as a clear indication that Khrushchev had chosen the West over China. Hostility between the two sides reached new verbal heights in the remaining months of 1963 in the exchange of open letters between the two Central Committees.

Still there were attempts at reconciliation. Boundary negotiations took place in Beijing in 1964. The Chinese side stated that the treaties relating to the frontier, though 'unequal' in nature, should be taken as the basis for settlement of the boundary question. The Soviet side, however, insisted that China recognize as belonging to the Soviet Union all the Chinese territory which it had occupied in violation of the treaties. As a consequence of this fundamental disagreement – which exists to this day – the negotiations were deadlocked.

On 15 October 1964 it was announced that Khrushchev had been ousted as premier and first secretary of the CPSU, and on the following day the Chinese announced that they had tested their first nuclear device. This two-day period thus saw substantial changes in the Sino–Soviet equation. The personal animosity and competition for leadership of the international socialist movement between Mao and Khrushchev, which had developed as relations between the two sides became more strained, would no longer be a factor in the Sino–Soviet relationship. Furthermore, China had now to be counted as a nuclear power. In yet another attempt to improve relations, Zhou Enlai travelled to Moscow, but it was not a propitious time for reconciliation as Mao was preoccupied with combating 'revisionism' within the CPC. In any event, Zhou did not find the new Soviet leaders any more disposed to compromise with Beijing than had been Khrushchev.

Increasing tension over the Vietnam War, and whether China and the Soviet Union should engage in 'united action', soon became the focus of Sino–Soviet relations. Beijing decided to prohibit Soviet aid by air to Vietnam passing over Chinese territory, and Moscow complained that even overland transport was obstructed. Mao firmly rejected Soviet proposals for united action and in March the Chinese Central Committee turned down Moscow's invitation to attend the 23rd Congress of the CPSU. Mao explained that China did not wish to be reliant on the Soviet Union. He said that henceforth any congratulatory tele-grams for such congresses would be sent only to the Soviet people, thus severing Party-to-Party relations. In April Washington and Beijing signalled to each other their intentions to contain their conflict in Vietnam, thereby improving one axis of the great-power triangle, just as the Sino–Soviet one reached a new low. Soviet leaders were now in a position to level charges of Chinese–American collusion. The tables were beginning to turn.

One of the most significant events shaping and consolidating China's new world outlook was the Soviet invasion of Czechoslovakia in the summer of 1968. Chinese criticism of Moscow could not have been more swift or more severe. In a speech at the Romanian embassy in Beijing on 23 August, Zhou Enlai accused the Soviet Union of trying to create puppets with the help of guns and compared the Soviet 'act of aggression' with Hitler's past invasion of Czechoslovakia and with US aggression against Vietnam.[12] The Brezhnev doctrine, asserting the right of the Soviet Union to take military action against any member of the socialist community, was announced shortly thereafter, with a clear relevance for China. Beijing was particularly infuriated by the corollary doctrine of 'limited sovereignty' which stated that the 'community' of socialist states – led, of course, by the Soviet Union – had the right to determine the destiny of any community member. Beijing denounced this as an 'outright doctrine of hegemony'.

On 2 March 1969 fighting broke out over Zhenbao (Damansky) island in the Ussuri river. From 1960 on there had been numerous smaller incidents, but this was the first serious clash between Soviet and Chinese forces, resulting in heavy Soviet casualties. On 15 March, Soviet forces attempted to recapture the island, and in this second encounter loss of life was even higher. In the spring and summer, clashes continued to take place along the Manchurian and Xinjiang borders and on 28 August an editorial appeared in *Pravda* referring to the possibility of an all-out Sino–Soviet war – a clear warning to the Chinese. On 11 September Premier Alexei Kosygin, returning from the funeral of Ho Chi Minh in Hanoi, stopped in Beijing for talks with Zhou Enlai. According to the Chinese, these airport conversations resulted in an agreement for an immediate ceasefire and withdrawal of troops. That such an agreement had been reached was subsequently denied by Moscow and the bickering went on. An agreement to hold talks on border questions was finally reached on 7 October, and the talks were convened in Beijing on 20 October.

This brief historical analysis makes it possible to identify several factors which contributed to the development of the Sino–Soviet con-flict. These can be grouped into three broad categories.

1. *State-to-state differences.* First, the Chinese realized, especially in the

aftermath of the Korean War, that Soviet economic 'aid' was to have strings attached and was little more than normal trade between the two sides. Second, the Chinese believed that the Soviet Union was unreliable as an ally. This was based on the Soviet failure to fulfil alleged promises to provide a sample atomic bomb and the technical information necessary for the production of nuclear weapons. It was also based on the Soviet failure to use its military power to support China in its attempt to gain control of Taiwan and in furthering the international aims of the socialist bloc. From the Soviet point of view, China came to be a liability in security terms: both reckless in support of its own interests and unrealistic in terms of what the Soviet Union could achieve in its struggle with the West. It was not so much that Moscow and Beijing differed in their ultimate assessment of US power, but rather on what tactics should be adopted – whether confrontation or competitive coexistence. The territorial issue, which was brought into the open in early 1963, was dramatically underscored by the border clashes of spring and summer 1969.

2. *Party-to-Party differences.*   These focused on the proper way to handle 'contradictions within the Party and between Parties'. The denunciation of Stalin was criticized by Chinese leaders as going too far: Beijing also resented open criticism of its domestic development policies by the Soviet Union, economic sanctions against Albania and Soviet interference in the internal affairs of fraternal socialist states.

3. *Personal differences.*   The personal animosity between Mao and Stalin and especially between Mao and Khrushchev often aggravated already important policy disagreements.

Since 1969 there has been no resolution of the border question; the treaty of friendship has been allowed to lapse with no new agreement to take its place. But nor has there been any major clash between the two sides since their representatives sat down in Beijing in October 1969, and in October 1982 Soviet ministers opened talks in China. Where are Sino–Soviet relations going?

Although the bilateral Sino–Soviet relationship has not markedly changed in the period from 1969 to 1982, there have been significant changes in the international environment. What is more, the world view of Chinese leaders, which had a profound impact on earlier Sino–Soviet ties, is also in flux. In the first half of the 1970s Chairman Mao met with President Nixon and then with President Ford, and significant steps were taken towards Sino–American normalization. Meanwhile, East–West relations were moving towards détente. By 1976, however, hopes for the success of détente were already beginning to fade.

In January 1976 Zhou Enlai died, and Mao's death followed in

September. In October the Gang of Four were arrested and China embarked upon a new political course. Mao's death seemed to afford Beijing new political and ideological options, both in domestic and international affairs, and the Kremlin was quick to react to the changes. Moscow ceased its anti-Chinese propaganda in September and declared the readiness of the Soviet Union to hold talks on the settlement of the frontier question. Beijing's anti-Soviet propaganda, however, continued unabated, and a message of congratulations sent by Leonid Brezhnev to Hua Guofeng on his appointment as chairman of the Chinese Communist Party was rejected. Subsequent overtures have also been rejected by Beijing as 'words without deeds'. It might, therefore, appear that Sino–Soviet relations have remained static over the past decade. This is not the case.

State-to-state relations

The past ten years have seen little real improvement in state-to-state relations. Chinese leaders have not forgotten the suffering and hunger of the Chinese people during the 'two terrible years' following the withdrawal of Soviet experts in 1960, and they have little reason to believe the Soviet Union would prove a more reliable friend today than during the 1950s and 1960s. During the 1970s Chinese leaders sought to improve their ties of friendship with Western Europe, Japan and the United States. In August 1978 China signed a treaty of peace and friendship with Japan, and in December President Jimmy Carter announced the establishment of diplomatic relations between Beijing and Washington. The Sino–Soviet treaty of friendship, alliance and mutual assistance was allowed to lapse on 14 February 1980, and although Beijing agreed in the autumn of 1979 to hold talks on normalization of Sino–Soviet relations, these talks were disbanded in the aftermath of the Soviet invasion of Afghanistan in late December. Moscow, which had previously been accused of 'revisionism' for not actively pursuing the interests of international communism, now stood accused of 'hegemonism'. But this catalogue of difficulties is far from the full story. Sino–Soviet relations have shown some important signs of détente, with the renewal of talks in October 1982 being the most promising example.

There have been other positive developments. Sino–Soviet trade has increased since 1970, flights between Beijing and Moscow were reintroduced on 30 January 1974 and agreements regarding the navigation of border rivers have been reached. Most instances of agreement or conciliation are, however, more complex than they first appear, and to regard such sporadic events as the release by Beijing of Soviet helicopter pilots in December 1975 and the lifting of the blockade of the waterway around Heixiazu (Bear Island) by the Soviet Union in

December 1977 as heralding a Sino–Soviet rapprochement is to ignore the fact that fundamental differences between Moscow and Beijing – most notably the border question – remain unresolved.

The Sino–Soviet border negotiations which opened in Beijing on 20 October 1969 were deadlocked almost from the beginning. The disagreements which had plagued earlier discussions, in 1964, proved once again to be insurmountable. Beijing insisted on implementation of the airport agreement between Alexei Kosygin and Zhou Enlai – an immediate ceasefire; disengagement of the armed forces of both sides in the disputed areas, which Beijing took to mean a return to the troop levels and dispositions existing prior to 1964; and maintenance of the status quo along the border prior to a resolution of the border question through negotiations. Chinese leaders further insisted that the Soviet Union admit that it had gained much of its Far Eastern territory through 'unequal treaties' concluded under the Tsars, and Beijing wanted discussions confined to questions relating to the frontier. Soviet delegates denied the existence of an understanding between the two premiers and insisted that there were no disputed areas on the Sino–Soviet border. They proposed that the talks should be widened to cover diplomatic, trade and cultural relations between the two countries.[13]

Talks on the frontier problem were held in Beijing with a number of breaks until 1979. The Chinese, while demanding an admission that the treaties imposed on them in the nineteenth century were 'unequal', were willing – as in 1964 – to take them as the basis for redefinition of the border. The Soviet delegates proposed, however, that in addition to the treaties the negotiations should take into equal account the historical development of the border areas and actual possession. The Soviet Union would thus retain the territory it held in accordance with the treaties by right of the treaties, the territory it had occupied in the century after the treaties were concluded by right of 'historical development', and the territory it had occupied since the boundary question developed in the early 1960s by right of 'actual possession'.

In 1971 the Soviet delegation tried a different approach and proposed a treaty renouncing the use of force. This was rejected by the Chinese side as unnecessary, since at that time the treaty of alliance remained in force. Moscow again offered in June 1973 to sign a non-aggression pact with China, but Beijing rejected all such proposals as pointless unless the Soviet Union carried out the agreement of 11 September 1969 to withdraw its forces from disputed areas. Following the rejection of this second offer Mr Leonid Ilyichev, the leader of the Soviet delegation, returned to Moscow and Leonid Brezhnev declared that Soviet attempts to normalize relations had failed because of China's openly anti-Soviet policy.[14] In October 1974 the Soviet government repeated its offer for a non-aggression pact between the two countries, but

Chinese leaders continued to make acceptance conditional on military disengagement in the disputed border areas.

Mr Ilyichev returned to Beijing to resume the border negotiations on 12 February 1975. Before his departure for Moscow in May, an agreement was apparently reached that the border problem should be examined item by item, beginning with those on which there was a greater chance of agreement. But despite this agreement and the release of the three crew members of the captured Soviet helicopter on 27 December 1975, both countries continued their propaganda campaigns against each other until Soviet leaders decided on a lull in their anti-Chinese statements following the death of Mao on 9 September 1976.

There was no break in Beijing's anti-Soviet propaganda, but Leonid Ilyichev was given a warm welcome when he returned to Beijing on 28 November to resume border talks after a break of 18 months. He left again on 1 March 1977, having failed to achieve progress in the deadlocked negotiations, and on 9 March, in response to a message from the Presidium of the Supreme Soviet of the USSR proposing talks to normalize relations, Beijing once again repeated preliminary conditions unacceptable to Moscow. In another forum, however, there was significant progress. The 20th regular meeting of the Sino–Soviet Joint Commission for Navigation on Boundary Rivers was held from 27 July to 6 October 1977 to discuss specific problems on the Amur and Ussuri rivers. The Soviet side decided to lift the blockade of the main channel around Heixiazu (Bear Island). The gesture may have been nothing more than a practical expedient since silting further upstream, turning the main navigational channel on to a course between the Chinese bank and a Chinese-held island, had given China the opportunity to apply reciprocal pressure by implicitly threatening a counter-blockade.[15] Still, it did at least display a determination on both sides to resolve problems peacefully rather than risk another military confrontation.

In the summer of 1978, as Washington and Beijing were moving towards normalization of relations, the Kremlin issued a sharp attack on China, warning 'short-sighted Western politicians' not to be fooled by friendly overtures from Beijing, and on 12 August another of Moscow's fears was realized with the conclusion of the Sino–Japanese treaty of peace and friendship. The growing friendship and economic partnership between the two great Asian powers fuelled Moscow's anxiety about encirclement. Deng Xiaoping travelled to Japan in the autumn, and during his trip he gave notice of Beijing's intention to allow the Sino–Soviet treaty of friendship and alliance to lapse.

On 3 November 1978 the Soviet Union signed a 25-year friendship treaty with Vietnam. On 7 January 1979 Vietnamese-led forces captured Phnom Penh. In mid-February Chinese troops moved into Vietnam, ostensibly 'to teach the Vietnamese a lesson' for provocations along the Sino–Vietnamese border. On 3 April Beijing formally announced that it would not extend its friendship treaty with the Soviet Union, but at the same time called on Moscow to join high-level negotiations to improve their relations. On this occasion Chinese leaders attached no preconditions, and on 23 September 1979 normalization talks – which were not to take the place of the stalled border negotiations but were to proceed as a separate forum – were convened in Moscow. On 9 October Beijing announced that the talks had been stalled since their start because the two sides had been unable to agree on an agenda, and at the end of November the first round of talks ended. No significant progress had been made and early in the new year Beijing announced that while Soviet forces remained in Afghanistan resumption of the normalization talks was inappropriate. In October 1982 the trend once again became more positive as Ilyichev returned to Beijing, apparently to resume the delayed negotiations.

There can be little doubt that many aspects of Sino–Soviet state-to-state relations remain severely strained. By virtue of the simple geography of two large bordering states with relatively difficult frontiers to defend, this uneasy hostility seems natural. These natural problems (unlike the similar US–Canadian border) are aggravated by rivalry for great-power status and leadership of the communist world. Thus to expect any return to the Sino–Soviet détente of the 1950s is to hope in vain. The Sino–Soviet honeymoon was an aberration in history, not the norm. However, it is equally fallacious to be mesmerized by the tendency of both communist powers to shout at each other. Even in state-to-state relations, important improvements have taken place.

It will be recalled that the major focus of state-to-state differences in the past was a disagreement on attitudes towards the capitalist West. These distinctions between Moscow and Beijing no longer have much basis. Indeed, it is now the Chinese who maintain better relations with the United States, and the Soviet Union has justification in claiming vindication for its policy of competitive coexistence. Some have argued that Sino–Soviet differences in their assessments of the capitalist West are as strong as ever, only it is now China that is following the path to détente. However, the recent Chinese shift to a more equidistant attitude to both superpowers suggests that such an assessment is no longer valid. With Beijing's line on Latin America, the Middle East and Africa more anti-American and less anti-Soviet than it has been in years, it is difficult to suggest that China and the Soviet Union have any major differences of opinion on the need to restrain US policy. Undoubtedly these alterations in the great-power triangle are not yet fully developed and are always subject to further alteration. But it remains clear that on the state-to-state level there are signs of change in Sino–Soviet relations.

Party-to-Party relations

Mao told Kosygin when he last saw him in 1969 that it might be possible to improve state-to-state relations, but that inter-Party ties would be much harder to ameliorate. The contemporary reality in Party relations is more complex, and, as at the state level, some signs of change are visible. In early November 1979 the CPC circulated an important document to officials that concluded that the Soviet Party should no longer be viewed as revisionist. The document said that the main threat from the Soviets was military expansionism, a reference perhaps to reports of the growing Soviet involvement in Afghanistan. In early April 1980 an article in the *People's Daily* repudiated the so-called 'Nine Commentaries' which had underscored the CPC's rift with the CPSU in 1963 and 1964, and which had labelled the Soviet Party 'revisionist' because of its emphasis on the development of productive forces. At about the same time, Anti-Revisionism Street in Beijing, on which the Soviet embassy is located, reverted to the name it had before the Cultural Revolution – North Centre Street.

It is apparent that with the rise of Deng Xiaoping and his allied economic reformers, it would be hypocritical in the extreme for China to castigate the Soviet Union for revisionism when China itself had chosen to travel the same road. Once again, analysts in Moscow must be struck by China's adoption, albeit belatedly, of many of the Soviet ideas of economic management. It will be recalled that it was precisely on this ground of differing domestic models for economic development that much of the inter-Party rows were fought. It is remarkable the extent to which both Moscow and Beijing have ceased attacking each other on internal economic issues.

While this aspect of improving Party relations is obvious, it is far more difficult to make sense of another key change in Chinese policy – the improvement of relations with Eurocommunists. It will be recalled that the 'Yugoslav heresy' was another key aspect of the original Sino–Soviet split and yet now Yugoslavia is a leading model for Chinese economic reform. Precisely those 'liberal' European communist parties that were the focus of so much Chinese vilification are now finding new friends in Beijing. Of course what unites many of the Eurocommunists and China is merely the belief that Moscow should not be allowed to dominate the world communist movement. On this important issue China and the Soviet Union remain far apart, but more in practice than theory. Nevertheless, there are also key areas where Moscow and Beijing do see eye to eye, even if the Eurocommunists do not. It is notable that China supported the imposition of martial law in Poland, not because the Soviet Union wanted it, but rather because it was a Polish solution to a Polish problem. The result was a coincidence of views between Moscow and Beijing on an aspect of Party relations.

This is not to say that there is any imminent improvement in Party ties. In April 1980 CPC Secretary-General Hu Yaobang made it clear that important obstacles blocked any such improvement. But, equally, it is inaccurate to suggest that there has been no change in Party-to-Party relations. Certainly the ground has been prepared for a resumption of talks about Party ties if the political will should emerge. What is most apparent is that the change in Sino–Soviet relations on the Party level, as on the state level, has more to do with changes in the Chinese line. The Soviet position has been relatively static on most dimensions of their bilateral relations, with China undergoing the policy gyrations. With perhaps yet another set of such acrobatics under way in Beijing, further change might be expected.

Personal relations

As noted before, the personal acrimony between Chinese and Soviet leaders – first between Mao and Stalin and later between Mao and Khrushchev – was partly a result of the intractible nature of the emerging differences between Moscow and Beijing.

Chinese propaganda lashed out at 'Khrushchev revisionism' while Moscow viciously attacked 'Maoist adventurism', but despite the efforts of Zhou Enlai, relations between Moscow and Beijing did not improve after the passing of Khrushchev from the scene, and despite Soviet hopes of better relations in the post-Mao period, Beijing did not respond favourably to Soviet overtures. In September 1976, after the death of Mao, Soviet leaders decided on a lull in anti-Chinese propaganda. Beijing did not reciprocate, and in April Soviet press attacks on China were resumed.

Chinese propaganda was, however, directed less against particular Soviet leaders in the post-Khrushchev period. Soviet propaganda in the post-Mao period has continued to attack 'Maoism' and has argued that 'de-Maoization' was a myth, but personal attacks on Chinese leaders have been rare. Thus, although Khrushchev's ouster and Mao's death did not lead to improvement in Sino–Soviet relations, they provided 'moments of opportunity' which for one reason or another were not seized upon, and they did perhaps result in a diminution of the importance of the personal factor in the dispute.

Since Beijing's hostility did not seem to be directed against Leonid Brezhnev personally but rather against Soviet policies, it seems unlikely that his passing will result in any significant change in the Sino–Soviet equation – unless, of course, it also results in policy changes which make the moment of opportunity more meaningful. Moscow's anti-Chinese propaganda now generally stops short of the kind of personal criticism previously levelled against Chairman Mao, and frequently attributes Chinese reluctance to resolve differences to remnants of Maoism'. Soviet leaders seem to hope thereby to avoid antagonizing elements of the Chinese leadership which might be more inclined to support Sino–Soviet normalization and which may eventually be powerful or influential enough to shape Beijing's policy. In the final analysis, the policies are more important than the personalities in Sino–Soviet relations. But as the first months of the Andropov regime made plain, changes in leadership can frequently give the historical process a 'shove' towards important change. It should, however, be recalled that the Sino–Soviet détente of the early Andropov era is merely a continuation of that of the final days of the Brezhnev era.

Change or continuity?

Although there have been developments and changes in state, Party and personal relations, there has been no major breakthrough. Sino–Soviet talks may result in a modest improvement in trade and some reduction of tension along the border, but a substantial improvement of relations remains unlikely, even if the United States persists in its '$1\frac{1}{2}$' China policy.

On the other hand, armed conflict between the two sides is equally unlikely. The Kremlin might once have thought in terms of a preemptive strike against China's nuclear facilities, but such an opportunity was never more than a fleeting and far-fetched notion. Neither does either power have much interest in a direct conventional military clash. Chinese leaders are unlikely to engage in adventurism. They know that the Soviet Union is not a 'paper tiger' and the People's Liberation Army, chastened by its engagement with Vietnam in 1979, is not likely to be spoiling for a fight.

Thus it is unlikely that the Soviet Union and China are about to 'kiss and make up'. It is equally unlikely that they will come to physical blows. The media will continue of course to seize upon every insult and signal. Every Soviet overture and friendly statement will be regarded as something new and momentous heralding rapprochement. Every incident on the border and every disagreement between Beijing and Moscow will revive fears of war. But important policy options remain between these extremes, any combination of which might have an important impact on Soviet policy. Sino–Soviet relations must remain the most crucial aspect of Soviet policy in the Far East, and thus Moscow will seek avenues for improving its position. Success or failure is only in part in the Soviet Union's own hands. In trying to deal with changing Chinese policy, Moscow is unlikely to find any simple exits from the maze that is Sino–Soviet relations.

Notes
 [1]   Harrison Salisbury, *The Coming War Between Russia and China* (London, Pan, 1969).

[2]   John Gittings, *Survey of the Sino–Soviet Dispute: A Commentary and Extracts from the Recent Polemics 1963–1967* (London, Oxford University Press, 1968), p. 43.

[3]   For the Soviet statement of the economic terms of the agreement, see Oleg Borisov and Boris Koloskov, *Soviet–Chinese Relations, 1945–1970* (Bloomington, Indiana, Indiana University Press, 1975), pp. 64–71.

[4]   J. Gittings, *Survey of the Sino–Soviet Dispute*, p. 56.

[5]   'The origin and development of the differences between the leadership of the CPSU and ourselves – comment on the Open Letter of the Central Committee of the CPSU', *People's Daily*, 6 September 1963, quoted in J. Gittings, *Survey of the Sino–Soviet Dispute*, p. 61.

[6]   J. Gittings, *Survey of the Sino–Soviet Dispute*, p. 90.

[7]   Ibid.

[8]   *Pravda*, 5 November 1962, quoted in Alfred D. Low, *The Sino–Soviet Dispute: An Analysis of the Polemics* (Rutherford, N.J., Fairleigh Dickinson University Press 1976), p. 126.

[9]   'The Open Letter of the Central Committee of the Communist Party of the Soviet Union to Party organisations and all communists of the Soviet Union', *Pravda*, 14 July 1963, quoted in J. Gittings, *Survey of the Sino–Soviet Dispute*, pp. 181–3.

[10]   *People's Daily* editorial, 8 March 1963, referred to in A.D. Low, *The Sino–Soviet Dispute*, pp. 181–2; the 'unequal treaties' are the Russo–Chinese treaties of Argim (1858), Peking (1860) and Ili (1881).

[11]   A.D. Low, *The Sino–Soviet Dispute*, p. 145.

[12]   J. Gittings, *Survey of the Sino–Soviet Dispute*, pp. 256–60.

[13]   *Keesing's Contemporary Archives*, p. 24691.

[14]   *Keesing*, pp. 26389–90.

[15]   Neville Maxwell, in *The Times*, 29 September 1978, and *The Hindu*, 30 September 1978.

The Soviet Union and the United States
J. David Armstrong

The United States is not an east Asian power, and so why is a chapter on the United States included in a book about Soviet east Asian policy? The answer lies less in the United States' geographic position, and more with its superpower status. Both superpowers share the uncommon characteristic of being powers in east Asia, but not east Asian powers.

The superpower relationship in east Asia has its roots in the events of the much neglected Asian Cold War. As in Europe, both superpowers met in east Asia as victors in the Second World War, and to an important extent their power in the area continues to be derived from the complex relationship with local states established at that time. Therefore it is with the roots of superpower conflict, and the intricacy of local policies, that this analysis must begin.

The origins and development of the Cold War in east Asia

In the last months of 1944 specific Allied preparations for an eventual Soviet entry into the war against Japan were made. Roosevelt had already given Stalin a strong hint at the December 1943 Teheran conference that the Soviet Union could expect to be rewarded for its aid against Japan, and Stalin is said to have returned to Moscow declaring that the Soviets '. . . had to utilize the favorable international situation to regain everything that Japan had grabbed as a result of the Russo–Japanese War'.[1] But when Stalin first spelt out detailed Soviet terms for entry into the Pacific war, in a discussion with Averell Harriman, US ambassador in Moscow, on 14 December 1944, he went somewhat further than the recovery of the Russian losses in the 1904–5 war with Japan. In the 1905 treaty of Portsmouth that brought the war to an end Russia had been obliged to cede the southern half of Sakhalin island and to transfer Russia's interests in Manchuria to Japan. But in his talks with Harriman, Stalin made it clear that his terms were now based on broader strategic calculations concerning the control of the Sea of Okhotsk and protection of Soviet lines of communication with

Vladivostok. As well as the continuation of an independent Outer Mongolia, the return of south Sakhalin, the lease of the Chinese Eastern Railway in Manchuria and the lease of Port Arthur and Dairen in China's Liaodong peninsula, he also wanted sovereignty over the Kurile islands, a chain of small islands which stretched for 700 miles between north Japan and the Soviet peninsula of Kamchatka.[2] These had been freely handed over to Japan as part of a territorial exchange in 1875.

This was the Soviet negotiating position on the post-war settlement in east Asia that faced US policy-makers in January 1945 as they prepared for the crucial Yalta conference. The broad outlines of US objectives in the region had been clear for some time. Public opinion needed to be satisfied both that the military threat from Japan was removed and that the sacrifice of US lives had brought some prospect of a post-war order that was more congenial to US ideals and more open to US economic power than the pre-war colonial order had been. A strong, united, pro-American China had for some years been the major pillar of the US design for east Asia, while Japan was envisaged as progressing under US tutelage towards a peaceful, democratic and capitalist future. France and the United Kingdom were seen as gradually relinquishing their colonial possessions and privileges throughout Asia. But in 1945 China was weak and divided, with the Nationalist government facing a strong challenge from the communists. The only genuine local power that was available to balance a resurgent Japan was the Soviet armed forces. Moscow's role was critical for another reason: if it were to back the Chinese communists in their fight with the Nationalists, this could lead to a potentially catastrophic Soviet–American confrontation and leave the US east Asian design in ruins. Thus quite apart from the perceived need to reach an agreement with Moscow in order to bring the Soviet Union into the Pacific war, there were compelling reasons for acknowledging the reality of Soviet power in east Asia and trying, if possible, to associate Moscow with Washington's hoped-for post-war order.

This was generally accepted in a US State Department briefing paper for Yalta that was drawn up in January 1945. US long-range policy was 'based on the belief that the need for China to be a principal stabilizing factor in the Far East is a fundamental requirement for peace and security in that area'.[3] And friendly relations between the Chinese and Soviet governments were a vital ingredient of this policy:

We regard Sino–Soviet cooperation as a *sine qua non* of peace and security in the Far East and seek to aid in removing the existing mistrust between China and the Soviet Union and in bringing about close and friendly relations between them. We would interpose no objections to arrangements voluntarily made by China and the Soviet Union to facilitate the passage of Soviet trade through

Manchuria, including the possible designation by the Chinese Government of a free port.[4]

On Korea, whose future had not yet been discussed with the Soviet Union in any detail, the State Department felt that it should come under some sort of international trusteeship to prepare it for eventual independence, with the US playing 'a leading role in the occupation and military government'.[5] But the Department was also anxious to qualify in various ways US support for the Soviet Union's territorial demands. It noted that the US navy wanted a base on the Kuriles, although these could still be under Soviet sovereignty. More seriously, it proposed that Japan should retain the southern Kuriles, with the remaining islands becoming a UN trusteeship under Soviet administration.[6] A similar arrangement was envisaged for south Sakhalin.[7]

At Yalta Stalin, showing a remarkable concern for the domestic constraints on him, insisted that the Soviet people and Supreme Soviet would not understand a declaration of war on Japan, 'a country with which they had no great trouble', unless his 'political conditions' were met.[8] Roosevelt may not have fully studied the State Department's papers[9] or he may simply have believed that Stalin would have found them unacceptable. For whatever reason, he conceded south Sakhalin and the Kuriles without question, but in the case of the Soviet request for the restoration of its rights and privileges in China, he insisted that Chinese agreement should be sought first and he also successfully urged Stalin to conclude a treaty of friendship with the Chinese government. Although Korea was discussed at Yalta, only a vague understanding was reached that it would come under an Allied trusteeship for a time.[10] However this was not included in the secret agreement signed after the conference in which the leaders agreed that the Soviet claims should be 'unquestionably fulfilled' after the defeat of Japan.[11]

The Yalta agreements provided a reasonably sound basis for an eventual post-war settlement in the Far East, but within months both major powers had developed strong suspicions about each other's intentions in the region. These were in part a reflection of tension between the two over European matters but there were a number of problems which arose independently in east Asia. One difficulty was that the Yalta accord left a number of questions unanswered. The future status of Korea was one of these but of more immediate importance was the fact that no precise policies had been worked out for the post-war occupation of Japan. During the war the Americans had become increasingly determined to keep control of the occupation exclusively in their hands but their allies were not made fully aware of this until after the end of the war. A further problem was that as US confidence in the certainty of Japan's defeat grew, so an increasing number of important policy-makers began to question whether Soviet entry into the war was still necessary.[12] Averell Harriman raised this issue on 12 April 1945, asking also what the US response would be to a Soviet request to participate in the occupation of Japan proper.[13] Navy Secretary James Forrestal went a stage further on 1 May when he enquired whether the United States was going to need a counterweight to Soviet influence in the Far East and if so whether China or Japan might be best fitted for the role.[14] Finally, there was considerable confusion in some quarters as to the exact contents and implications of the Yalta agreement. As late as 13 July the State Department had no copy of it or record of the discussions at Yalta.[15] More seriously President Truman was unsure about Roosevelt's full purpose in signing the agreement on the Far East and about any informal understandings as to the precise meaning of some of its clauses.[16]

At the July Potsdam conference there was a Soviet–American clash over the exact nature and extent of the Soviet sphere of influence in China which had been promised at Yalta. Within a few days of the Japanese surrender Truman and Stalin gave themselves fresh grounds for suspecting the other's intentions in the Far East. On 16 August Stalin requested a Soviet occupation zone on Hokkaido (in Japan proper) as well as the inclusion of all the Kurile islands in the Soviet zone.[17] Truman in reply rejected the request for Soviet troops to be stationed on Hokkaido and countered with a proposal for US air-base rights for commercial and military purposes on the Kuriles. Stalin replied in outraged tones that the latter request was of a kind 'usually laid before either a conquered state, or such an allied state which is in no position to defend certain parts of its own territory.' Truman, who may have been merely attempting to revive the idea for a Kuriles base that had been aired in the State Department's pre-Yalta briefing document but which had not previously been mentioned to the Soviets, sent Stalin what he saw as a 'mildly conciliatory reply'. But one passage in it may have seemed to Stalin to contain an implied threat: 'I was not speaking about any territory of the Soviet Republic. I was speaking of the Kurile Islands, *Japanese territory, disposition of which must be made at a peace settlement*' (emphasis added). Although Stalin decided not to take this matter any further, he must have been disturbed at the clear implication – however hypothetical – that the Soviet territorial gains which had been agreed at Yalta could still be lost at a subsequent peace conference. On the US side concern was expressed from an early stage that the Soviets intended to impose a communist regime on Korea.[18] Hence portents of a Soviet–American confrontation had appeared in all three east Asian countries before the end of August 1945.

A recent Soviet publication discusses the United States' Far Eastern policy in 1945 in terms which suggest that basic strategic considerations ray have been at the root of Soviet perceptions of US and of Moscow's own policies in the region. US policy-makers under Truman are depicted as gradually abandoning Roosevelt's policy of preserving good relations with Moscow and instead working for a post-war situation in which the power of the pro-American Chiang Kai-shek was preserved in China, a capitalist Japan was built up under US tutelage and a government established in Korea that was dependent on the United States and capable of blockading the southern exits from the Sea of Japan.[19] Such a policy, it was maintained, would have had the effect of building around the Far Eastern possessions of the Soviet Union a military belt that was 'anti-Soviet in its political base'.[20] That these suspicions were made known at the time to Washington is clear from a number of telegrams sent from Moscow by Averell Harriman.[21] However, in one of these, on 16 October, Harriman asked for urgent clarification as to what US Far Eastern policy actually was, which suggests that the latter was by no means as clearly worked out as Moscow seems to have suspected. Indeed the true picture was that opinion was deeply divided at the highest levels of US policy-making over the best US approach to Far Eastern affairs (at least with regard to China and Korea; there was broad agreement on Japan). In the case of Korea, the commander of the US occupation forces in the south was urging 'positive action' to resist Soviet activities in the north from as early as November 1945.[22] On the other hand, the official State Department position in 1946 was that

basic US objectives with regard to Korea can only be attained through agreement with the Soviet Union. In fact, the policy problems raised by Korea assume added significance because they entail the necessity of agreement with the Soviet Union and thus become part of the much more vital problem of relations between the US and the Soviet Union.[23]

A similar difference of views emerged in June 1946, when President Truman's special adviser, Edwin Pauley, wrote after a visit to the Far East that Korea was 'an ideological battleground upon which our entire success in Asia will depend. It is here that a test will be made of whether a democratic competitive system can be adapted to meet the challenge of defeated feudalism, or whether some other system i.e. Communism will become stronger.'[24] But in his reply to Pauley, Truman suggested instead that the promotion of liberal reforms in Korea might help to broaden the basis for an understanding with the Soviets.[25]

US policy in China during the late 1940s was similarly marked by the absence of a clear, widely supported view of what the true situation there was, what precisely US objectives were and what resources Washington should be prepared to devote to attain them. There were greatly differing interpretations of such crucial matters as Soviet intentions, the nature of the Chinese Communist Party and its relation ship with Moscow, and the advisability of sustaining the Chiang Kai shek regime. Indeed Soviet policies themselves were marked by some ambivalance, in contrast to their approach to North Korea, where the Soviet occupation forces had immediately set about installing a communist regime dominated by Koreans who had been living for several years in the Soviet Union. In the case of China there were well-justified Soviet suspicions about the reliability of the Chinese Communist Party, as well as a tendency to waver between minimalist objectives, such as a substantial economic presence in a weak and disunited China,[26] and the maximalist goal of a communist China which, however, carried with it certain possible dangers for the Soviet Union that may have been perceived at the time. But what both superpowers had certainly acquired from an early stage was a readiness to suspect each other's motives in the Far East.

Hence, quite apart from the impact on east Asia of the general deterioration in Soviet–American relations, there were particular factors inhibiting an understanding between the two in that region. Therefore, in July 1947, when Washington called for a peace treaty to be concluded with Japan but insisted that it should be negotiated by the 11 members of the Far Eastern Commission, where decisions were made by a two-thirds-majority vote, it was inevitable that Moscow (perhaps recalling Truman's August 1945 note to Stalin) should assume that this was a plot to deprive it of its Yalta gains and refuse to participate unless it had a veto. However, the official US attitude at this stage, while certainly designed to safeguard its nearly exclusive control over Japan, was not necessarily as hostile to the Soviet Union as it may have appeared to Moscow. One member of the State Department actually complained that the United States was *not* utilizing the peace settlement to further its security interests against Moscow. Arguing that the central US objective 'is taken to be a stable Japan, integrated into the Pacific economy, friendly to the US and, in case of need, a ready and dependable ally of the US', he protested that the US draft peace treaty 'appears to be preoccupied with drastic disarmament and democratization under continued international supervision, including the USSR'.[27]

Even as late as 1948, George Kennan could still hope for an eventual 'general understanding with the Russians relating to the security of the northwestern Pacific area'.[28] What made this impossible was the overall worsening of the Cold War, the 'loss' of China to Mao's communists, the North Korean invasion of South Korea, the outbreak of paranoid hysteria in the United States itself and Washington's decisive shift towards the policy, long urged by some, of treating Japan as a major ally rather than a potential enemy. These events have been exhaustively discussed in many studies. Here it is sufficient to note their impact on superpower perceptions of each other in east Asia.

Although the possibility that Mao might become an 'Asian Tito' had been frequently mooted in the State Department, Secretary of State Acheson was quick to conclude that Mao's victory meant that the communists 'have foresworn their Chinese heritage and have publicly announced their subservience to a foreign power, Russia'.[29] The 'hard-line' view of Moscow as the fountainhead of a worldwide aggressive conspiracy was enshrined in the famous National Security Council document (NSC 68) which was drafted in April 1950 and called for 'a rapid and sustained build-up of the political, economic and military strength of the free world', together with an 'affirmative program' to wrest the initiative from Moscow.[30] In Asia the NSC had earlier defined as a basic US objective the 'gradual reduction and eventual elimination' of what was (wrongly) seen as 'the preponderant power and influence of the USSR' and called for a programme of US aid and support for regional organization.[31]

There was by no means universal acceptance of the analysis and prescriptions embodied in NSC 68 but the Korean War helped to silence critics since it could be portrayed as proving the central point of the document: that communism was a monolithic and inherently aggressive force.[32] Although not yet enunciated in such terms, a 'domino theory' of Asia began to prevail in Washington in which any prospect of a communist takeover had to be countered wherever it occurred since it was regarded as a threat to neighbouring states. The United States began to build up its network of alliances and other commitments in Asia, which eventually embraced Japan, South Korea, Taiwan, the Philippines, Pakistan and Indochina, as well as Australia and New Zealand. Thus the Korean War established the pattern for Soviet–American relations throughout the 1950s and beyond, and it also set the United States on the course which led to the Vietnam War.

In retrospect there is, of course, strong reason to doubt the accuracy of both the general NSC appraisal of Soviet power and intentions and the interpretation of the Korean War which stemmed from this kind of thinking. This is not to say that the Soviet Union was ever the peace-loving innocent featured so touchingly in its own propaganda, but that it may have proceeded from a basis of cautious opportunism rather than a predetermined design for world domination and that it may have been more constrained by various domestic factors than was generally realized.[33] In the particular case of Korea, the origins of the North Korean decision to attack the South now appear far more complex than was appreciated at the time. The original view of this decision was that it was arrived at during the two-month period when Mao Zedong was in Moscow negotiating the Sino–Soviet alliance treaty. In 1950 Mao and

Stalin were seen by Washington as indistinguishable so far as the responsibility for this decision was concerned while the North Korean leader, Kim Il-sung, was regarded as a mere cypher. Later there was some debate over whether Mao was more responsible than Stalin or *vice versa*.[34] However, in Khrushchev's memoirs he asserts 'the war wasn't Stalin's idea but Kim Il-sung's. Kim was the initiator. Stalin of course didn't try to dissuade him . . . Mao Tse-tung also answered affirmatively.'[35] Later he relates that Stalin recalled all the Soviet military advisers in North Korea just before the invasion, arguing that 'we don't want there to be evidence for accusing us of taking part in this business. It's Kim Il-sung's affair.'[36] Others have supported the contention that North Korea enjoyed considerably more independence than was realized in 1950.[37] But such views should not be pressed too far: there can be little doubt that Stalin was capable of restraining Kim had he so wished. However, on this occasion he may have simply miscalculated, seeing the possibility of important strategic gains with apparently minimal risk and misreading various US signals which had seemed to exclude Korea from the US 'defensive perimeter'.

The emergence of the great-power triangle in east Asia

From the Soviet perspective, one of the most ominous developments in the aftermath of the Korean War was Washington's evident determination to build up Japan as a countervailing force to Soviet power in the Far East. In 1951 the San Francisco peace treaty with Japan was concluded by 49 states, not including the Soviet Union which refused to sign since it had been unable to obtain any of a large number of demands which it had made relating to Japanese reparations, the demilitarization of Japan, the removal of US bases, Soviet sovereignty over all of the Soviet-occupied Japanese territories, the closure of the Sea of Japan to non-litoral states (i.e. the United States) and the ending of various restrictions which had been placed on the activities of the Japanese Communist Party.[38] Shortly after the peace treaty was signed, Japan and the United States signed a security treaty and in March 1954 an additional mutual defence agreement was concluded. From that time onwards Washington consistently encouraged Japan to devote more resources to its own defence. An additional blow for Moscow came when the US Senate, in ratifying the peace treaty in 1952, added a proviso which effectively called for the restoration to Japan of the Kuriles and south Sakhalin.[39]

The Soviet response to these events, after an initial show of belligerence, was to seek to normalize its relationship with Japan as a first step towards weaning Japan away from a rigid alignment with US foreign policy. Despite US pressure on Japan to resist Soviet blandishments, Moscow was able on 19 October 1956 to agree a joint declaration with

Japan which formally ended the state of war between them and established diplomatic relations. But a proper peace treaty was unobtainable because Tokyo continued to press its territorial claims which Moscow was unwilling to grant. However, economic relations improved steadily following a trade agreement in December 1957. Thereafter bilateral trade increased a hundred-fold, reaching 2,600 million roubles in 1979.[40]

Until the 1970s, the only significant period of strain in the continuing Japanese–Soviet normalization came in 1960 when a revised US–Japan security treaty was agreed at a time when Soviet–American relations had reached a low point because of the shooting down of a US U–2 spy plane over Soviet air space. The treaty, according to Moscow, meant that 'Japan's foreign policy and, in the final analysis, its destiny are bound up with the US adventuristic policy directed against Japan's neighbours. The US–Japanese treaty is turning Japan into a willing or unwilling accomplice in the US aggressive policy in the Far East.'[41] But this dispute did not prevent a continuing expansion of commercial relations throughout the 1960s to a point where the Soviet Union was a major supplier to Japan of cotton, timber, nickel, copper and other raw materials and a leading market for a range of Japanese exports, including machine tools, steel pipes and certain types of rolling stock.[42]

It is possible that one of the reasons why the Soviet Union adopted a harsh line towards Japan in 1960 was the impact of its increasingly acrimonious dispute with China. Both Moscow and Bcijing were vying for the support of the Japanese Communist Party, which was strongly opposed to Japan's close relationship with the United States.[43] Later the target of both China and the Soviet Union tended to be the Japanese government rather than the Communist Party and a contest developed between the two communist giants to develop the closest rapprochement with Japan. This was one of the important triangular relationships which developed in north-east Asia during the 1960s and 1970s. The other, of course, was that involving China, the Soviet Union and the United States.

The public emergence of the Sino–Soviet dispute in the early 1960s had surprisingly little impact at first on the image of monolithic, aggressive communism which underlay US foreign policy in Asia. Instead of being seen as puppets of a joint Sino–Soviet dictatorship, the small Asian communist states of North Vietnam and North Korea were now depicted as being essentially the vanguards of Chinese expansionism in Asia. If anything, some US policy-makers were inclined to see a possible community of interests with the Soviet Union in Asia, especially after Moscow had failed to give wholehearted support to China during the Taiwan straits crisis of 1958 or China's dispute with India, which developed during 1959. US propaganda had for years portrayed China as a uniquely evil and aggressive nation and it was not easy to reverse positions overnight.[44] However, during 1966 there were a number of small signs that Washington might be considering improving its relations with Beijing as a means of giving itself greater flexibility at a time when it was becoming more and more heavily embroiled in its Vietnam disaster.[45] But the Vietnam War itself tended to freeze international relationships in east Asia for a few years, while the upheavals in China as a consequence of its Cultural Revolution effectively removed any prospect of a sensible Chinese approach to foreign relations during the 1966–9 period.

A remarkable coincidence of interests enabled China and the United States, which had hitherto depicted each other in ferociously antagonistic terms, to achieve a more rapid reversal of positions than either had thought possible. Washington wanted to reduce its increasingly heavy worldwide strategic burden but without, if possible, opening up fresh opportunities for Moscow. As Richard Nixon's 'Guam doctrine' of 1969 had indicated, there was a particular desire to limit the United States' commitments in Asia. Most immediately, the United States wanted a way out of Vietnam and a rapprochement with China could possibly assist in this goal, either through China's own links with North Vietnam or as an extra form of leverage on Moscow to use its influence with Hanoi.[46] Beijing itself had been experiencing a deepening sense of insecurity vis-à-vis Moscow ever since the Soviet invasion of Czechoslovakia in 1968. In 1969 conflict broke out at several points along the Sino–Soviet border and Moscow issued several indirect threats about the possibility of a preemptive strike being launched against Chinese nuclear installations.[47] Confronting both superpowers simultaneously was clearly becoming an impossible option for China.

Henry Kissinger is insistent that the rapprochement with China was not seen by Washington as 'inherently anti-Soviet'.[48] Unsurprisingly, this was not the view from Moscow – indeed it could not possibly be since an improvement in Sino–American relations would ipso facto at the very least impose an additional constraint on Moscow without bringing it any corresponding gain. Indeed Kissinger's own account includes a memorandum to Nixon which acknowledged as much: 'Pressure on the Russians is something we obviously never explicitly point to. The facts speak for themselves.'[49] He also states that well before his famous 1971 visit to China was even contemplated, he and Nixon 'alone among senior policymakers' were convinced that the United States would not be able to accept a Soviet military assault on China.[50] This effectively gave the relationship something of the character of an informal security alliance.

Initially, however, Moscow's response to Washington's China initiative was not unduly hostile. The US policy since Korea of isolation and non-recognition of China had always been an unnatural posture, and normalization as such, while it complicated matters, need not necessarily pose serious problems for Moscow. And while the conduct of US foreign policy was in the hands of Nixon and Kissinger, who had committed themselves to the pursuit of détente with the Soviet Union, there were grounds for hoping that Washington would refrain from 'playing the China card' too frequently. As one Soviet analyst writing in 1980 saw it:

For a number of reasons the United States displayed a certain restraint for quite some time in developing its relations with China. There was a struggle in Washington's government circles between supporters of the 'policy of keeping equidistance' from the USSR and China that took into account the need to continue detente in relations with the Soviet Union, and supporters of the policy of accelerating rapprochement with Peking even at the price of certain concessions to it in the Taiwan problem and giving assistance to China's arming against the USSR.[51]

In the aftermath of Nixon's resignation in 1974, Sino–American relations entered a less harmonious period, with frictions developing largely because of the United States' continuing relationship with Taiwan, with whom total US trade in 1976 reached US $4.8 billion, as against a low point of only US $336 million with China.[52] In the same year Mao died and Moscow for a time ceased its polemics against China in an unsuccessful bid to encourage a shift away from the virulently anti-Soviet policies that had been associated with Mao.

Although it was the most dramatic east Asian event of the 1970s, the Sino–American rapprochement was not the only development of interest. Indeed, in terms of military links and trade, Japan remained by far the most important US connection in the region, especially in the aftermath of the US withdrawal from Vietnam. Japanese leaders had been profoundly shaken by the 'Nixon shocks' of 1971 (the opening to China and the floating of the dollar). Japanese feelings of vulnerability increased with the oil crisis of 1973 and Tokyo began cautiously to pursue a more independent line in its foreign policy. For a period in the mid-1970s, it found itself being courted simultaneously by Moscow, Beijing and Washington, albeit for very different reasons.

The US objective throughout the 1970s was to encourage Japan to increase its spending on defence which would enable the United States itself to reduce its defence burden in the Far East and in all probability lead to a larger Japanese role in Asian security generally. In particular, Washington was anxious to obtain a significant Japanese commitment to the defence of South Korea. But on the Japanese side there was some uncertainty, in the wake of the communist victories in Indochina, as to the United States' willingness and ability to go to war, if necessary, on behalf of its remaining Asian allies. The Japanese defence White Paper of 1976 noted that the military balance between the United States and the Soviet Union in Japan's region had shifted decisively in favour of the Soviet Union during the 1965–75 period.[53] Moreover the US commitment to South Korea seemed to be weakening, especially after the mid-1970s 'Koreagate' allegations that the South Korean government had been involved in the bribery of members of the US Congress. President Carter came to office with plans for the withdrawal of US ground forces in South Korea, another cause for alarm in Japan. Finally, Japan's massive trade surplus with the United States was a further source of irritation. In 1977 US trade with the Pacific region was, for the first time, greater than its trade with Europe.[54] But in that year the US deficit in trade with Japan rose to around US $8 billion.[55] This led to what one observer described as 'the most serious bilateral crisis since the occupation'.[56] In December 1977 the two sides agreed on a package of measures to improve the situation, but by 1982 the US deficit had reached a projected US $16 billion and a new phase of economic friction was under way.[57] However, although economic relations were generating tension in this way, there was some progress on the strategic front as a result of a period of intensive diplomacy in 1975, whose success enabled President Ford to declare on 7 December 1975 that 'partnership with Japan is a pillar of our strategy. There is no relationship to which I have devoted more attention.'[58] One result for this diplomacy was the setting up of a new consultative body for defence cooperation. But despite some small increases in Japanese defence spending, US officials remain unconvinced that the 1 per cent of Japanese GNP devoted to defence amounts to a reasonable Japanese contribution to regional security.

1978 and after: détente or a new Cold War in Asia?

In 1982 a Soviet analyst of Chinese affairs wrote: 'The course towards a military and political rapprochement of the United States and China, with Japan increasingly drawn into the process, is designed to upset the existing strategic balance in the world. It is a serious threat to security and a new, dangerous development in international affairs.'[59] This reflected the Soviet concern that a number of developments from 1978 onwards had combined to create a potentially threatening situation for Soviet interests. The most ominous of these came in August 1978, with the signing of the Sino–Japanese peace and friendship treaty, which was seen by Moscow as anti-Soviet in its implications. Japan had hitherto pursued a policy of equidistance between Moscow and Beijing and each power had for some time been attempting to induce Tokyo to enter into a closer relationship with it, which would include, in the Soviet case, a formal peace treaty still awaiting conclusion. The treaty that Tokyo was eventually persuaded to sign with China included a clause opposing 'hegemony' – Beijing's codeword for the Soviet Union. Tokyo's decision was taken partly because Moscow, while on the one hand offering Japan rich economic prospects in exploiting Siberia, had on the other appeared to adopt a more menacing posture in its response to Japan's claim to four of the northern islands seized by the Red Army in 1945. At one time Moscow had seemed to be willing to concede at least part of Japan's claim but during 1977–8 Soviet officials responded in harsh and implacable terms to the territorial claim and also to the question of Japanese fishing rights in Moscow's newly proclaimed 200-mile exclusive economic zone around the islands.[60] The Soviet Union also stepped up its naval activity in the region and began to fortify some of the islands.

Moscow may have initially hoped that the Sino–Japanese rapprochement would not proceed too far. Soviet analysts stressed that China was not proving as reliable and attractive a trade partner as the Japanese had hoped, that its oil was of inferior quality and that Japan's economic interest in the continuing existence of an independent Taiwan was a source of contention, as was the dispute between China and Japan over the ownership of the Senkaku islands.[61] Similar hopes about possible future frictions were expressed in relation to Japanese–American economic 'contradictions', with the much greater complementary nature of the Japanese and Soviet economies strongly emphasized.[62] But what one writer has called 'the great transformation'[63] in east Asia during 1978 and afterwards continued in ways that generally carried adverse implications for Soviet interests. Japan's 1978 White Paper on defence explicitly named the Soviet Union as Japan's potential enemy for the first time.[64] President Carter decided to slow down the US troop withdrawal from South Korea and at the end of 1978 he announced the formal US recognition of China. Soviet observers also thought they detected signs from 1978 onwards of increasing pressure in Japan for the acquisition of a more significant military capacity, even including nuclear weapons and Cruise missiles.[65]

It may have been partly in response to these perceived pressures that Moscow made a number of initiatives in 1978–9 which, however, had the effect of sharpening Japanese, Chinese and US apprehensions and causing them to draw closer together. These Soviet moves included the signing of a virtual treaty of alliance with Vietnam in November 1978, which was quickly followed by Vietnam's invasion of China's ally, Cambodia, and China's retaliatory attack against Vietnam. Then, in late 1979, the Soviet Union invaded Afghanistan and triggered off a series of US-inspired sanctions against it. Japan loyally supported Washington in these sanctions, even to the extent of seeing its position as the Soviet Union's second largest trading partner slip to fifth place.[66]

The increasing glut of various kinds of raw material had, in any case, reduced the Soviet Union's economic attractiveness to Tokyo. Washington also responded by strengthening its links with China. During a visit to Beijing in June 1981, Secretary of State Haig announced that the United States was now prepared to sell arms to China on the same case-by-case basis governing US arms transfers to all other nations.[67] Further measures in this direction were taken in December 1981. Soviet alarm about this trend was expressed by Soviet Defence Minister Ustinov on 22 June 1981: 'The US Administration has not ceased its attempts to set up new aggressive military–political blocs and alliances, in addition to the old ones. The Washington–Peking–Tokyo triangle has recently acquired increasingly clear outlines of an aggressive alliance in the Far East.'[68] Moscow also demonstrated some concern about proposals for the creation of a larger Pacific Community which would have primarily economic purposes but also some military and strategic implications.[69]

During 1982 Moscow appeared to show some appreciation of the fact that it was, in part, its own heavy-handedness that had caused the disturbing situation that now confronted it in east Asia – where even its North Korean friends seemed to be tilting significantly towards China, and where Sino–Japanese trade had reached double the level of Soviet–Japanese trade. Moscow found it difficult to soften its line on the Soviet–Japanese territorial issue and continued to call for greater Japanese independence from the United States as well as for what President Brezhnev termed 'a sober approach on the part of the Japanese side to the realities that have taken shape as a result of the Second World War . . .'[70] But in other aspects of its policy in east Asia signs of flexibility began to appear. For instance from mid-1979 some cautious gestures were made towards developing a more normal relationship with South Korea, a state with which the Soviet Union had had no links whatever prior to 1970.[71] But of far greater importance was a major initiative on 24 March 1982 by Brezhnev to improve relations with China. The Soviets had been trying since late 1981 to persuade Beijing to reopen talks about the border dispute which had been broken off by the Chinese in the wake of the Soviet invasion of Afghanistan. Then, in his March speech, Brezhnev made a strong call for a restoration of friendship between the two: 'we well remember the time when the Soviet Union and People's China were united by bonds of friendship and comradely cooperation. We have never considered the state of hostility and alienation between our countries to be a normal phenomenon.'[72] Brezhnev mentioned Soviet proposals for 'confidence-building measures in the Far East that could lessen tensions and strengthen peace' and, for good measure, also called for similar discussions with Japan. The Soviet offer was reiterated on a number of ccasions and in October 1982 a high-level Soviet delegation went to Beijing to commence discussions.

The Soviet initiative was clearly made in the hope of taking advantage of frictions between China and the United States that had appeared since the presidential inauguration of Ronald Reagan in 1981. Some members of Reagan's administration had expressed scepticism about China's realistic significance in the overall balance of power, while Reagan himself, during his presidential campaign, had hinted at the possibility of the US relationship with Taiwan acquiring some quasi-diplomatic status.[73] The continuing US sales of arms to Taiwan became a major bone of contention between Washington and Beijing during 1981. In January the two sides began negotiations in an effort to resolve their differences and Brezhnev's proposals were made amid reports that these talks were encountering difficulties. But Soviet hopes were to some extent dashed in August 1982 when the Sino–American talks managed to achieve a basic framework of agreement on the Taiwan question. In essence the agreement committed the Americans to a gradual reduction of their arms sales to Taiwan, while China indicated that it would pursue the goal of ultimate reunification with Taiwan through peaceful means.[74]

A further setback for Moscow had occurred earlier in August 1982 when Tokyo for the first time approved an increase in its defence spending to a level greater than 1 per cent of Japan's GNP.[75] This was still substantially less than Washington would have liked to see the Japanese spend on defence but it continued a trend of recent years that carried disturbing future implications for the Soviet Union. If the inhibitions in Japan against developing a significant military capacity were ever to weaken, it would have an extremely destabilizing impact on the east Asian balance of power: a defence spending of 5 per cent of GNP would put Japan well above British or French levels. Although as yet only a very distant prospect, the combination of this with the possibility of a steadily improving Chinese economic base must form the far from reassuring long-term background against which Soviet policy will be framed.

As for the US view of the east Asian situation in the middle of 1982, this was given in a statement by Walter J. Stoessel, Jr, deputy secretary of state, before the Senate Foreign Relations Committee on 10 June.[76] He saw the east Asian and Pacific region as having grown enormously in its economic importance and as likely to continue to do so. General Soviet objectives were regarded as strategic in nature: 'to seek positions of maximum geopolitical strength from which to project power and influence'. Specific aims were to neutralize Japan in any conflict, weakening existing defence ties and ultimately isolating Japan. The build-up of Soviet military power in the Kuriles was seen as enabling it to overlook strategic sea lanes linking the seas of Japan and Okhotsk with the northern Pacific. This would enable Moscow to interdict supplies of Middle Eastern oil to Japan at times of crisis and deny east Asian routes of access to the Indian Ocean to the United States. Other Soviet objectives included an attempt to limit external assistance to China's modernization efforts by exploiting trade links to discourage Western Europe and Japan from close economic and defence ties with China.

In discussing the contribution of east Asian nations to US regional security objectives, Stoessel praised Japan's new approach of 'comprehensive security' – combining political, economic and military measures to strengthen Japan's own security and develop links with other strategically important states. But he indicated that Washington still found Japanese defence spending to be too low. He made a strong commitment to South Korea, adding that although the US–Republic of Korea alliance was aimed only at deterring aggression from the north, this had a larger significance in Washington's broader objectives vis-à-vis the Soviet Union in east Asia. Finally China was described as 'a friendly, nonallied country with which we share important strategic interests, including a common perception of threatening Soviet ambitions worldwide'. It played an important role by tying down Soviet and Vietnamese troops and by supporting the US military presence in the region.

Conclusion

In February 1947, when a US interdepartmental committee was deliberating US options with regard to Korea, it concluded that if the United States recognized an independent South Korea but simultaneously withdrew American forces, 'it would be obvious to the world that the US had suffered a complete political defeat in a test of strength with the Soviet Union in the only area where we and the Soviets stand face to face alone'. Furthermore, if Moscow attained a dominant position in Korea, 'The loss of US prestige and influence, and the consequent increase in Soviet influence and power, would have prejudicial repercussions not only on US interests in the Far East but on the entire US world position.'[77]

At about the same time Moscow was advancing a similarly bleak view of world affairs which divided all states into two camps and anticipated a struggle to the end between them. On both sides international relations were depicted as a 'zero sum game', where any gain by one side was automatically a loss to the other. Such rigid certainties tend to create their own reality which in turn confirms the belief that gave rise to it. This has certainly been the experience in east Asia, particularly in the case of US policy, although the Soviet Union has shown itself to be equally unyielding in the face of perceived threats. Indeed the danger of conflict in the future will stem less from US initiatives than from Soviet disregard for the interests and apprehensions of other regional powers. For example, Moscow's attempt to improve relations with Beijing is likely to fail unless the Soviet Union can understand how threatening some of its recent behaviour, and that of its allies, appears in China. Likewise, relatively small concessions could produce significant gains in the Soviet relationship with Japan. But concessions are not part of the rules of zero sum games.

Notes
[1] N.N. Voronov, 'The exploitation of the Soviet people', *Istoriya SSSR*, no. 4 (July–August 1965), pp. 13–27, cited in D.S. Clemens, *Yalta* (New York, Oxford University Press, 1970), p. 59.

[2] *Foreign Relations of the United States* (hereafter *FRUS*): *The Conferences at Malta and Yalta*, 1945 (Washington, DC, 1955), pp. 378–9.

[3] Ibid., p. 356.

[4] Ibid., pp. 356–7.

[5] Ibid., p. 360.

[6] Ibid., pp. 382–3.

[7] Ibid., pp. 387–8.

[8] Ibid., p. 769.

[9] R.L. Messer, *The End of an Alliance: James F. Byrnes, Roosevelt, Truman and the Origins of the Cold War* (University of North Carolina Press, 1982), p. 41.

[10] *FRUS: The Conferences at Malta and Yalta*, p. 770.

[11] Ibid., p. 984.

[12] A. Iriye, 'Continuities in US–Japanese relations, 1941–49', in Yonusuke Nagai and Akira Iriye (eds), *The Origins of the Cold War in Asia* (Tokyo, 1977), pp. 389–92.

[13] W.A. Harriman and E. Abel, *Special Envoy to Churchill and Stalin 1941–46* (New York, Random House, 1975), p. 461.

[14] W. Millis (ed.), *The Forrestal Diaries* (New York, Columbia University Press, 1951), p. 52.

[15] *FRUS: Conference of Berlin (Potsdam)*, 1945, p. 864.

[16] R.L. Messer, *The End of an Alliance*, pp. 67–70.

[17] H.S. Truman, *Memoirs*, vol. 1 (New York, Signet, 1965), pp. 485–90, contains this correspondence; see also *FRUS*, 1945, vol. 6, pp. 667–70.

[18] *FRUS*, 1945, vol. 6, pp. 689–90.

[19] *Mezhdunarodnye Otnosheniya na Dal'nem Vostoke* (Moscow, Progress Publishers, 1978), vol. 1, p. 30.

[20] Ibid.

[21] For example, *FRUS*, 1945, vol. 6, pp. 754–5, 849–51.

[22] Ibid., p. 1106.

[23] *FRUS*, 1946, vol. 8, p. 697.

[24] Ibid., pp. 706–9.

[25] Ibid., pp. 713–14.

[26] J. and G. Kolko, *The Limits of Power* (New York, Harper & Row, 1972), p. 263; and G. Warner, 'America, Russia, China and the origins of the Cold War', in J.M. Siracusa and G. St John Barclay (eds), *The Impact of the Cold War* (New York, 1977), p. 150.

[27] Memorandum by John P. Davies of the Policy Planning Staff, 11 Aug. 1947, in *FRUS*, 1947, vol. 6, pp. 485–6.

[28] G.F. Kennan, *Memoirs 1925–1950* (Boston, Little, Brown, 1967), p. 393.

[29] *United States Relations With China* (Washington, DC, Department of State, 1949), p. xvi.

[30] *FRUS*, 1950, vol. 1, pp. 234–92.

[31] *FRUS*, 1949, vol. 7, pt. 2, p. 1215.

[32] W. La Feber, *America, Russia and the Cold War* (New York, Wiley, 4th edn, 1980), p. 100.

[33] There was in fact something of a debate during 1951 between Charles E. Bohlen and the NSC over precisely these questions; see *FRUS*, 1951, vol. 1, pp. 106–9, 163–75, 177–8, 180–1.

[34] See, e.g., M.D. Shulman, *Stalin's Foreign Policy Reappraised* (Cambridge, Mass., Harvard University Press, 1963), p. 141, and A.B. Ulam, *The Rivals: America and Russia since World War II* (New York, Viking, 1971), pp. 170–1.

[35] *Khrushchev Remembers* (Boston, Little, Brown, 1971), p. 368.

[36] Ibid., p. 370.

[37] For example, G. Warner, 'The Korean War', *International Affairs*, no. 1 (January 1980).

[38] R.K. Jain, *The USSR and Japan 1945–1980* (Brighton, Harvester, 1981), pp. 14–20.

[39] D.F. Lach and E.S. Wehrle, *International Politics in East Asia Since World War Two* (New York, Praeger, 1975), p. 159.

[40] V. Dalnev, 'Impediments to Soviet–Japanese relations', *International Affairs* (Moscow), no. 2 (February 1981), p. 49.

[41] Cited in S. Modenov, 'Tokyo: following Washington's lead', ibid., no. 5 (May 1981), p. 65.

[42] I. Kazakov, 'Soviet–Japanese economic relations', *Far Eastern Affairs* (Moscow), February 1976, pp. 73–9.

[43] G. Jukes, *The Soviet Union in Asia* (Berkeley, Calif., University of California Press, 1973), p. 189.

[44] R.P. Stebbins, *The United States in World Affairs 1965* (New York, Harper & Row, 1966), p. 32.

[45] R.P. Stebbins, *The United States in World Affairs 1966* (New York, Harper & Row, 1967), pp. 267–80.

[46] Henry Kissinger states that this latter aim was very much in Richard Nixon's mind. See *The White House Years* (London, Weidenfeld & Nicolson, 1979), p. 164.

[47] Ibid., pp. 183–6.

[48] Ibid., pp. 191–2.

[49] Ibid., p. 765.

[50] Ibid., p. 764.

[51] V. Petukhov, 'PRC–USA: a threat to peace and security', *Far Eastern Affairs* (Moscow), no. 3 (March 1980), p. 56.

[52] W. Watts *et al.*, *Japan, Korea and China* (Lexington, Mass., Heath, 1979), p. 107.

[53] W.J. Barnds (ed.), *Japan and the United States* (London, 1980), pp. 159–68.

[54] Saburo Okita, 'Japan, China and the United States: economic relations and prospects', *Foreign Affairs*, vol. 57, no. 5 (1979), p. 1091.

[55] C.F. Bergsten, 'What to do about the US–Japan economic conflict', ibid., vol. 60, no. 3 (1982), p. 1060.

[56] W.J. Barnds (ed.), *Japan and the United States*, p. 195.

[57] C.F. Bergsten, 'What to do about the US–Japan economic conflict'.

[58] *Department of State Bulletin*, no. 1905 (29 December 1975), p. 914.

[59] V. Semyonov, 'Beijing's hegemonism and international security', *International Affairs* (Moscow), no. 7 (July 1982), p. 20.

[60] W.J. Barnds (ed.), *Japan and the United States*, pp. 169–70.

[61] N. Vladimirov, 'Japan faces the 1980s', *Far Eastern Affairs* (Moscow), no. 1 (1980).

[62] V. Alexandrov, 'Siberia and the Far East in Soviet–Japanese economic relations', ibid., no. 2 (1982), pp. 21–32.

[63] S. Karnow, 'East Asia in 1978: the great transformation', *Foreign Affairs*, vol. 57, no. 3 (1979).

[64] D. Petrov, 'Militarisation of Japan is a threat to peace', *Far Eastern Affairs* (Moscow), no. 2 (1981), p. 50.

[65] Ibid., p. 51.

[66] *Far Eastern Economic Review*, 23 July 1982, p. 43.

[67] 'Developing lasting US–China relations', US Department of State, Bureau of Public Affairs (Washington, DC), Current Policy, no. 398 (1 June 1982).

[68] Quoted in 'Peace in Asia is a common concern of the continent', *Far Eastern Affairs* (Moscow). no. 1 (1982), p. 7.

[69] S. Nikonov, 'A new Pacific alliance in the offing?' ibid., no. 3 (1980).

[70] Quoted in V. Dalnev, 'Impediments to Soviet–Japanese relations', p. 50.

[71] Tae-Hwan Kwak, 'Recent Soviet policy toward the two Koreas', *Korea and World Affairs*, vol. 3, no. 2 (Summer 1979).

[72] Cited in I. Alexandrov, 'On Soviet–Chinese relations', *International Affairs* (Moscow), no. 7 (July 1982), p. 16.

[73] R.H. Solomon, 'East Asia and the great power coalitions', *Foreign Affairs*, vol. 60, no. 3 (1981), pp. 693–701.

[74] *Far Eastern Economic Review*, 20 August 1982.

[75] Ibid., 6 August 1982.

[76] US Department of State, Bureau of Public Affairs (Washington, DC), Current Policy, no. 403 (10 June 1982).

[77] *FRUS*, 1947, vol. 6, pp. 610–18.

5 The Soviet Union and Japan
Wolf Mendl

At the beginning of the 1980s, the outlook for Soviet–Japanese relations was as bleak as the storm-tossed waters around northern Hokkaido. The bilateral relationship, which had mellowed in the era of détente during the late 1960s and early 1970s, began to cool after the MiG incident of 1976[1] and became steadily frostier. No prospect of a thaw appears to be in sight, so that an essay such as this seems to offer little scope for anything other than an analysis and explanation of the deteriorating relationship and speculation over the depths to which it might yet fall.

However, such an approach would overlook the shifting and contradictory moods beneath the surface, the historical perspective of Russian–Japanese relations, and their international context. If we add these dimensions to the analysis, we may discover that the causes of the estrangement are to be found on both sides and that the adversary relationship, in spite of all appearances, need not be taken for granted.

Apart from economic interests, which are discussed elsewhere in the book, Soviet–Japanese relations are governed by three determinants. One is the dispute over the so-called Northern Territories (see Appendix, pp. 65–7)- a dispute which the Japanese place at the centre of their relationship with the Soviet Union and which the Soviets deny even exists.

Another determinant is the international environment in which the bilateral relationship operates. A glance at the history of the Russo–Japanese encounter in north-east Asia suggests that mutual antagonism has not always been its dominant feature. It is the impact of regional and global politics which has sharpened the confrontation and seems to make their differences all the more intractable today. Japan's association with the United States, the Sino–Japanese relationship, the problem of Korea, the strategic balance between the superpowers and the economic depression, all affect the course of Soviet–Japanese relations to a greater or lesser degree.

The third determinant is provided by the subtle atmospherics of the relationship, which are difficult to define. The attitudes of Japanese and Soviets towards each other and the emotional and psychological currents affecting them are important elements in the mutual appreciation of two peoples that are culturally and racially so different from each other.

The historical dimension

If we confine our view of Soviet–Japanese relations to the past few years, then we can only see a bedrock of irreconcilable attitudes. A longer view embracing the post-war era reveals a different picture in which periods of accommodation, as in the normalization process of the mid-1950s, leading to the joint declaration, signed in October 1956,[2] which ended the state of war between the two countries, and again during the Siberian development 'boom' of the late 1960s and early 1970s, alternate with periods of hostility, as in the early 1950s and late 1970s.

An even longer perspective, covering the history of modern Japan from the middle of the last century until the end of the Pacific War, reveals a similar pattern of swings between friendly and hostile relations. The era is usually seen as dominated by the Russo–Japanese War of 1904–5, but only 11 years later the two countries signed a secret agreement to assist each other in the event of a third party seeking to gain supremacy in China. Similarly, a year after the end of the Japanese occupation of Siberia (1918–22), a 'statement on imperial defence' identified the United States as the chief hypothetical enemy of the future and recommended a policy of good relations with Russia. By 1936 both were posited as potential enemies and the ambivalence reflected the differing perceptions of the imperial army and navy, which can be traced back to the early years of this century. Until the very last days of the Second World War the relations between Japan and the Soviet Union were governed by a neutrality pact, in spite of the fact that they were ranged on opposite sides of a conflict in which they were each at war with one another's partners.

The friction between the two countries can be explained very simply as the result of an inevitable clash of interests between two powers – one advancing into the east Asian region from Europe across Siberia and the other expanding beyond its island territories, partly in reaction to pressures from other imperialist powers. While Americans, British and French were knocking on Japan's doors from east and west, the Soviets were doing the same thing from the north.

Russia has always had a precarious hold over its vast territories in north-east Asia – the Russo–Japanese War and the Allied occupation of Siberia at the end of the First World War showed just how shaky its power was – and its primary interest was to secure its possessions through influence or domination over the countries on their borders: China, Mongolia, Manchuria, Korea. While the Russians sought to secure their position by further expansion in Asia and the manipulation of neighbouring states, Japan was engaged in a similar exercise to prevent rivals from extending their primacy over Korea and China and thus threatening Japan itself. No wonder that there were clashes between the two states, and the pattern continues to some extent to this day.

Soviet Russia inherited the Tsarist legacy. After a brief attempt to marry its ideology to reality, it settled into the role of a major power in the Far East, though one which was essentially defensive in orientation because of its exposed position at the end of a railway line 5,400 miles long. There were other reasons for its defensiveness: its main interest was in Europe; it was isolated in the world and felt ideologically beleaguered; and there was the folk memory of invading hordes from the east, going back to the days of Genghis Khan, reinforced in modern times by anxieties about the presence of China's teeming millions on the borders of its own empty and largely virgin lands.

That fear persists and expresses itself in such phrases as the 'Yellow Peril'. Its focus was on China, but Japanese penetration into China before the war and Japan's present economic relations with that country incline the Soviets to identify them with the 'Yellow Peril' as well. The Japanese, in turn, saw the Soviets as part of the European threat to their security. They were outsiders and, as such, aliens in east Asia. It would not be correct, however, to think that there was an unmitigated racial animosity towards them.

In some respects the Japanese acquired their view of the Russians from other Europeans, who have tended to regard Russia as an economically and culturally backward country which was none the less militarily strong and threatening. Furthermore, in school today they do not learn about the Japanese occupation of Siberia, but they do learn about the Nikolaevsk 'massacre' in May 1920, when about 700 Japanese were murdered by soldiers of the Red Army.[3] Most Japanese think that the problems of the current relationship with the Soviet Union started in 1945, with the violation of the neutrality pact, the seizure of the Northern Territories and the miseries of hundreds of thousands of Japanese prisoners of war in Soviet hands.

Yet, Japanese policy towards the Soviet Union has been variable and pragmatic in spite of such emotional predispositions. The Soviet Union is only one actor among several in the region and the Japanese interest is to neutralize the various powers by balancing them against each other. In the century before the war that policy led to periodic rapprochements between Japan and Russia. After 1945 there was first the close association with the USA in the face of a united front by the communist giants and then the attempt to be even-handed in dealings with the Soviet Union and China. Once the Soviet Union was perceived as a growing threat through the rapid expansion of its military strength in the 1970s and there were indications of a weakening US commitment to the region, Japan leant towards China in the hope that an emerging but weak China, an economically strong but militarily weak Japan and a still strong but weakening US presence would together balance the power of the Soviet Union. That is where the policy rests today and it is not surprising that the Soviets, in a mirror image of perceptions, should be worried about the formation of a Peking–Tokyo–Washington axis.

The issues

From the historical perspective, therefore, it is not a foregone conclusion that Japan and the Soviet Union are eternal enemies. This is also true when we consider the various elements that constitute the current bilateral relationship. Its economic aspect is dealt with by Kazuyuki Kinbara in Chapter 8 and we need here only note several features which give it a political significance.

The volume and value of bilateral trade may not amount to much when compared with Japan's total foreign trade, but are more significant when compared with Sino–Japanese trade. In the first half of 1981 the Soviet Union replaced China as the second largest export market for Japanese steel products.[4] In that year the value of Japan's trade with the Soviet Union rose by 13.8 per cent in comparison with 10.5 per cent for trade with China and 14.5 per cent for trade with the United States.[5] Japan is now the single most important market for Soviet timber and coal.

In the field of energy, the relationship is summed up in the words of an official US report:

Japan depends on the USSR for only a miniscule part of its energy supply. Similarly, Japan is the West's largest supplier of energy-related technology and equipment to the Soviet Union, yet these exports constitute a relatively small part of Japan's total world exports.[6]

The Soviet Union might have some slight leverage on Japan in so far as certain industrial interests, notably the steel industry and the fishery lobby, are opposed to the use of economic factors as points of pressure on Soviet policy. In the supply of sources of energy, the Soviets have no really effective instrument of pressure, but here the Japanese may have some leverage as suppliers of energy-related equipment and technology, for no matter whether the Soviets give priority to western Siberia or eastern Siberia, they are in need of this assistance. Their only room for manoeuvre is in playing off European suppliers against the Japanese, as they did over the issue of interest rates covering the cost of steel imports.[7]

Taking the economic element in the bilateral relationship as a whole, it has to be seen at least as a factor of restraint on the extremes of hostility and at most as a source of encouragement for more relaxed relations. It has been suggested that Japanese leaders regard joint energy development projects as an indication of their commitment to peaceful coexistence in Asia.[8]

On the other hand, this does not imply that they expect a great increase in the supply of sources of energy from the Soviet Union. Soviet economic strategy for the next decade is likely to concentrate on developing the oil and natural gas resources of western Siberia. Europe (East and West) will be the main partner and beneficiary of this development.[9] Japan can only expect to benefit from the sale of technology and equipment for the enterprise. The prospects of sources of energy from the Soviet Union are confined to the exploitation of the coal deposits in Yakutia and oil and natural gas off Sakhalin. In adopting this strategy, the Soviet Union encourages the Japanese to turn to China in their search for sources of energy and is thus creating precisely the kind of liaison that it is most anxious to prevent.

At the political level, the Japanese try to combine a policy of reassurance with a firm commitment to the West in general and the United States in particular, while the Soviets play contrasting tunes of threat and accommodation, of which the first tends to be the louder, reinforced as it is by demonstrations of naval and air power in Japan's vicinity.

The territorial dispute has become the main bone of contention in recent years, but the underlying and most important issue remains the security treaty system with the United States. I shall return to this below but must first address the question why the Japanese have chosen to push the Northern Territories into the centre of their relations with the Soviet Union.

The issue arose even before the ink on the San Francisco peace treaty was dry. Japanese of all political persuasions have never accepted the 'legitimacy' of the Soviet seizure of the islands. They regard the Soviet Union's entry into the war, a week before surrender and after Japan had sought its good offices to end the conflict, as a violation of the Soviet–Japanese neutrality pact of 1941 and as an act of treachery.

The US occupation of the Ryukyu islands could at least be justified as the outcome of a hard-fought war. No such justification existed for the Soviet occupation of the Northern Territories. Following the return of the Ryukyus to Japanese administration in 1972, the Soviet presence on the islands in the north has become even more of an insult and irritation.

It is a very complicated problem none the less: the case for the return of the Habomais and Shikotan seems irrefutable; that for the return of Etorofu and Kunashiri is more debatable. Whatever the interpretation of the geographical, historical and legal evidence, until the 1970s, at least, there appeared to be some room for compromise: the return of the Habomais and Shikotan and the prospect of a further review of the status of Kunashiri and Etorofu. The position of the two sides has hardened since 1976 and Japan's declaratory policy has made the unconditional return of all four the prerequisite for improved relations with the Soviet Union, while the latter insists that there is no territorial issue.

It is possible to advance several explanations for the impasse. One represents it as the result of a kind of historical momentum in which neither side can get off the hook. Any substantial change of position would appear to be a surrender to the other and would involve an unacceptable loss of face – a particularly important consideration for the Japanese who have just about come round to thinking of their country as one of the world's 'major' powers, whatever that may mean.

However, this explanation does not seem very convincing. It may be true in the current international climate but there is no reason to believe that it must continue once some new form of détente develops. After all, the Chinese waxed very hot and strong over their claim to the Senkaku islands[10] in the early 1970s and then agreed to shelve it indefinitely at the time of the treaty negotiations in 1978 and are even prepared to consider some form of joint exploration and exploitation of the resources of the surrounding seabed.

It is often said that even if the Japanese might be prepared to compromise in a mellower international climate, the Soviets could never surrender any territory because it would open a Pandora's box of claims from many other states on their borders. Apart from giving up attempts to detach Azerbaijan from Iran, the evacuation of the naval base at Porkkala in Finland, withdrawal from parts of Chinese Manchuria and withdrawal from their zone of occupation in Austria, they have not relinquished one square inch of territory in Europe or elsewhere since the war. Yet these examples show that the Soviets, too, can be very pragmatic when it suits them and they could return to their stance in 1956 on the grounds that, as certain conditions had been fulfilled, the Japanese could have back the Habomais and Shikotan.

The gradual militarization of the Northern Territories and the surrounding area is perhaps a more convincing explanation of the deadlock. The Soviets now have 1 division on the islands, 2 on Sakhalin, 1 in Kamchatka and more than 10 in the Maritime Provinces facing the seas of Japan and Okhotsk. Four Japanese divisions are located in Hokkaido.[11] The Soviet military build-up is probably defensive in purpose. For the time being, the Soviet Union has neither the air-nor the sealift capability to launch and sustain a major invasion of Hokkaido. Even the most likely scenario – a Soviet attempt to seize the Japanese shore of the Soya/La Pérouse strait on Wakkanai peninsula opposite Sakhalin – seems implausible.

The objective of placing military installations on the islands is to reinforce control over the Sea of Okhotsk and to protect the lines of communication with the major bases facing the Sea of Japan. They also guard the exits into the northern Pacific through the Kurile screen, making sure that the Japanese will not be tempted to make a sudden swoop on some of the islands with locally superior forces. In addition, one can see this as part of the Soviet Union's posture of warning to Japan, given the Soviets' propensity to believe that the language of force is the most effective in international relations.

In the light of Japan's defence arrangements with the United States and for as long as there is a US military presence in Japan and its immediate neighbourhood, it is most improbable that the Soviets would risk a limited or localized attack on Japan. Such an event is only likely to occur in a major international conflict including an armed clash between the superpowers. In those circumstances the Soviets would certainly not pull their punches. However, there is no evidence that they are deliberately preparing to launch hostilities in east Asia. What is known of their policies and strategies, their military capabilities and dispositions, points against such a course of action.

Moreover, they have some reason to be apprehensive. In the past several years the Japanese have become increasingly specific about the Soviet 'threat', which is spelt out in some detail in the most recent White Paper on defence.[12] Not only does it list possible scenarios for a Soviet attack, but it states unequivocally that the Self-Defence Forces (SDF) are to have the capability of blockading the four strategically important straits in the seas around Japan for the purpose of denying the Soviet Pacific fleet access to the China seas and the Pacific in the event of hostilities.

Officially, Japan regards Soviet military activities in the area as a potential but not an immediate threat. They are, however, seized upon by the defence establishment, politicians, and some industrial circles to focus public attention on the danger from the north. Anti-Soviet books and theses about the Third World War are best-sellers, especially in Hokkaido. At a Northern Territories rally in Tokyo, the secretary-general of the ruling Liberal-Democratic Party (LDP), later to become foreign minister, was reported to have described the construction of Japan–Soviet Friendship Halls in various parts of Hokkaido as 'definitely an act of indirect aggression'.[13] One could continue with other examples of this tendency to build up a mood of apprehension and anger over the Soviet 'threat'.

Those who lay stress on it do so from various motives, among which, of course, *genuine* anxiety plays a major part, and the Soviets, whether they want to or not, are doing their best to encourage it. But there can also be no doubt that the Soviet 'threat' is exploited by the Self-Defence Forces, particularly the ground forces, to justify their claim to a greater share of national resources and greater esteem in the public eye. It is used by industrial and commercial interests which, for various reasons, want to see the armaments industry receive a boost. And it is seized upon by nationalists who believe a militarily strong Japan is a good thing.

Shifting moods

If objective factors, such as economic data, military strength and deployment, formal agreements and various incidents are the dry bones of Soviet–Japanese relations, then interpretations of the intentions of the two parties and their mutual perceptions are the flesh and blood of the relationship. They provide the crucial dimension upon which its course ultimately depends.

The MiG incident is usually taken as the most recent turning-point in Russo–Japanese relations, marking the beginning of their steady deterioration. There had been plenty of irritations and difficulties before that, but it is possible to trace a continuous decline since. On the Japanese side there has been a steady escalation of the territorial issues, beginning in 1976 with Mr Miyazawa's 'inspection' of the islands from a safe distance, the first foreign minister to do so. Two years later the government began to promote tours for the public to 'view' the islands. In 1981 it decided to make 7 February Northern Territories Day, an annual event to commemorate the signing of the treaty of Shimoda (1855) which had set the boundary between Japan and Russia north of Etorofu. Also in 1981, a bill was laid before the Diet, incorporating six villages on Kunashiri, Etorofu and Shikotan into various communities in eastern Hokkaido. The Soviets played their part in exacerbating the issue by harassing fishing vessels in the vicinity of the islands and, since 1978, building up their military strength in the Northern Territories.

In addition to this central theme of discord, there have been numerous other events which have led to mutual recriminations: frequent overflight of Japanese air space by Soviet military craft; a spy scandal which broke at the time of the Soviet invasion of Afghanistan;[14] the business of salvaging the cruiser *Admiral Nakhimov*[15] and claiming it as a Japanese prize; the towing of a crippled Soviet nuclear submarine through Japanese waters in August 1980 without waiting for permission; and so on.

Some of these incidents were the result of Soviet action (overflights, the towing of the submarine through Japanese waters), others came from the Japanese side (the spy scandal which inflamed anti-Soviet feelings at a time when the government wanted to rouse public support over its stand against the Soviet occupation of Afghanistan, the claim to ownership of the *Admiral Nakhimov*). Yet, in the background of all this friction, there have been conciliatory notes in a minor key, in spite of the persistence of the Soviet Union's status among the Japanese as one of the countries they like least.

Until the signing of the Sino–Japanese treaty of peace and friendship in August 1978, the Japanese were at pains to stress their even-handedness in relations with the communist giants, symbolized in January 1975 by the simultaneous visits of Foreign Minister Miyazawa to Moscow and the elder statesman of the LDP, Shigeru Hori, to Peking. Feelers towards the Soviet Union continued to be put out after 1978 and the Japanese have insisted on their neutrality in the Sino–Soviet dispute. On 8 March 1981, Foreign Minister Ito tried to reassure the Soviet ambassador, Dmitri Polyansky, that Japan had no intention of ganging up with the United States and China.

The circumstances in which this meeting came about are a useful illustration of the hidden nuances of the bilateral relationship. Polyansky was a man of declining importance in the political hierarchy of his country. At the time of his appointment as ambassador to Japan in 1976, he had already lost his position as minister of agriculture and, more significantly, membership of the Politburo. He remained a member of the Party's Central Committee but, unlike his colleagues accredited to West European countries, he had never been recalled to participate in its plenary sessions. Add to this the tradition that once a Soviet politician has lost a leading position there is no likelihood of his return to power, and it becomes clear that the Soviet Union did not give a very high priority to its relations with Japan.

Polyansky, who had just lost his seat on the Central Committee, had originally asked for an interview with Prime Minister Suzuki. The tone of Japanese reactions varied. The foreign minister apparently struck a fairly gentle note in his conversation with the ambassador. The prime minister was studiously non-committal, but the chief Cabinet secretary, Miyazawa, was incensed and rude. The request had been unprecedented, especially as Polyansky had no new important proposals to put before the Japanese – the only reason why a meeting with the premier might have taken place. It was suspected that he wanted to reconnoitre Japanese attitudes on the eve of Suzuki's first encounter with President Reagan. Miyazawa accused the ambassador of not having bothered to study Japanese society and culture sufficiently.

The affair reveals a tendency among the Japanese to exaggerate Japan's importance in Soviet eyes and, on the other side, Soviet insensitivity to the importance of status in Japanese eyes. There were some who said that Polyansky was not even worthy of an interview with the foreign minister and no doubt the feeling of insult was heightened by the fact that Brezhnev had omitted to send the Japanese even a copy of a recent communication to West European heads of state.[16]

The continuing friction may obscure but does not obliterate the ambivalence of Japanese attitudes towards the Soviet Union. A recent example is the visit by ten LDP members of the Diet to Moscow in April 1981. All belonged to an intra-party group which exists to promote Japanese–Soviet friendship. On their return, their leader, Iichiro Hatoyama, a former foreign minister, urged Japan to follow 'its own policy' towards the Soviet Union instead of siding unreservedly with the United States in world politics. He also wanted the West to be more objective in its evaluation of Brezhnev's peace offensive at the February Congress of the CPSU.[17]

This softer line reflects important business interests, especially in the steel industry and in fisheries. One of the members of the LDP mission was the president of the Japan Fisheries Association. In spite of harassment,[18] Japanese fishermen have been quite successfully wooed by the Soviet authorities with special 'privileges' for those who are 'friendly'.[19] The city council of Wakkanai contributed towards the cost of a Russian–Japanese Friendship Hall, while the president of the Fishing Cooperative of Nemuro, the peninsula closest to the occupied Northern Territories, called on Japan to reduce its claim to two of the islands (presumably Shikotan and the Habomais) in order to reach a settlement with the Soviet Union.[20]

There exists, then, a substantial body of opinion in Japan that is not in full accord with the current hardline policy towards the Soviet Union; a body of opinion made up of a variety of economic and political interests. But the mainstream of opinion undoubtedly supports the official stand and its alignment with the US position over the Soviet 'threat'. Nevertheless, the government still feels constrained to emphasize its search for better relations with the Soviet Union. Thus, the Foreign Ministry proclaimed Northern Territories Day as a day to strive for Japanese–Soviet friendship in memory of the treaty of Shimoda![21]

Whether there are similar divergences in attitudes towards Japan within the Soviet political system is hard to tell. The present leadership is probably still influenced by the experience of the Second World War and pursues policies to impress on Japan that it lost the war. The message is rubbed in by the occasionally threatening tone when dealing with Japan. In 1978 there were threats of retaliatory action if Japan signed the treaty with China, and the fortification of the Northern Territories was justified as a response to that treaty. *Pravda* warned in

1980 that, in the event of a nuclear war, Japan might be subject to nuclear retaliation. On the other hand, the Soviet Union has also attempted rather clumsily to follow the conciliatory line. This was especially noticeable in the period leading up to the treaty with China when there were faint hints of flexibility over the territorial issue. They have disappeared completely since 1978, but the olive branch continues to appear occasionally amidst the usual tough-sounding language.

While the Soviet position over the territorial question has remained unaltered, there has been an attempt more recently to shift Japan from its generally uncompromising stand that nothing can be achieved without a territorial settlement. The passage in Brezhnev's speech at Tashkent on 24 March 1982, which is addressed to Japan, reiterated the theme of good neighbourliness, mutually beneficial cooperation and expanded economic relations which could result from the removal of 'a few hindrances created by external forces which care little about the interests of our two countries . . . [and which] have striven to prevent Japan from appearing on the world arena as an independent, sovereign state'.[22]

However, the only change in the Soviet stance has been to abandon the earlier proposals for an Asian Collective Security system and instead to offer a bilateral agreement. The idea was taken up at a Japan–Soviet Round Table Conference held in Tokyo in April 1982, which, though private, was attended by the Soviet marine transportation minister and prominent Japanese politicians. It accepted most of the Soviet theses on bilateral relations and on arms control, and opposed the policy of economic sanctions. But the meeting failed to achieve a union of minds on the territorial dispute, even though the Japanese side only asked the Soviets to accept the existence of a problem, as stated in the joint declaration of 1956.[23]

In urging Japan to recognize political realities and 'the facts' created by the war, the Soviet Union clearly hopes that eventually there will be a settlement on the lines of the agreements between the Federal Republic of Germany and the Soviet Union and other East European countries, recognizing the post-war frontiers. There may be little prospect of Japan's agreeing to such an arrangement, but Brezhnev's reference to external forces preventing it from becoming an 'independent, sovereign state' sought to exploit the current wave of national self-assertion, reinforced by growing irritation at the high-handed US policy over economic sanctions, which is threatening progress on the Sakhalin oil and natural-gas project.

One can dismiss all this as mere tactical ploys, but they may also reflect an uneasiness over Japan's role in east Asia and an anxiety to prevent it from becoming completely absorbed in an anti-Soviet front. It is possible that there is a debate among Soviet policy-makers between

:hose who subscribe to the belief that the Japanese only understand the
language of force and those who believe that Japanese neutrality, if not
friendship, can be won by a more accommodating approach that offers
some, albeit minor, concessions.

The international environment

The current international environment encourages the rising ride of
anti-Soviet sentiment in Japan although there are also some countervailing forces. The government is caught between these cross-currents.
Some of its members incline to the former view and favour a much
stronger stand and accelerated rearmament. Others prefer the 'softly
softly' approach. A third group favours a continuing dialogue with the
Soviets, but only within the limits permitted by Japan's commitment to
the United States. It is the interpretation of this commitment which
very largely dictates the course of Japan's policy towards the Soviet
Union. The present state of superpower relations, not to mention
encouragement from China and Soviet behaviour towards Japan, has
created a temporary coalition between those for whom Japan's alliance
with the United States is the overriding consideration in Japan's foreign
policy and those who make the creation of a 'strong' and eventually
more independent Japan their most important objective.

Some time in the future, the paths of these two schools may diverge
and it need not be a foregone conclusion that Japan's attitude towards
the Soviet Union will remain set in an aspic of hostility. For the present,
however, Japan is embedded in the agreement between Washington
and Beijing over the Soviet 'threat'. Hence the more positive aspect of
Japanese–Soviet relations, i.e. economic cooperation, is kept low-key,
while the negative aspect, notably the territorial dispute, tends to be
stressed, albeit with repeated professions of the desire to have friendlier
relations with the Soviet Union. To some extent this reflects the exigencies of domestic politics and in particular the continued ascendancy of a
pro-China mood. Most important, however, is the wish to impress the
United States.

The Japanese are embarrassed and increasingly irritated by a constant stream of criticism from across the Pacific, often reinforced by
complaints from the other major industrialized states, that Japan trades
unfairly, that it is waxing prosperous at its friends' expense, that it is
enjoying a 'free ride', that it does little for the security of the West and
to counter the threat from Soviet expansionism. Given the general
consensus[24] that Japan must rely on the treaty with the United States
for its basic security, the current emphasis on an unfriendly and potentially dangerous Soviet Union serves two purposes: it demonstrates to
the United States and the other Western powers that Japan is no
appeaser and can be counted upon to stand firm against the Soviets and

it helps to create a mood among the people which would make them more receptive of a greater defence effort.

This is not, of course, to deny that there are *real* points of friction between Japan and its northern neighbour and that the Soviets are at least as much to blame for the current bad relations. But the persistent undertone of readiness to mend fences with the Soviet Union and the existence of important groups which would welcome such a development suggest that the pragmatic and flexible Japanese, unfettered by the ideological blinkers of the present administration in Washington, might under certain circumstances modify their stand.

Such circumstances might include a cooling of Sino–American relations, accompanied by a partial restoration of friendly relations between the Soviet Union and China and a generally more independent policy on the part of China vis-à-vis both superpowers, of which there have been some indications recently. Alternatively, the relationship between China and the United States might become much closer, once the present little difficulty over Taiwan is resolved. Such a development might have important implications for Japan's interests in China and relegate the Japan–US security system to secondary importance in the eyes of the Americans. Again, it is not inconceivable that détente between the superpowers might come about again and that they would agree on a condominium of the world rather than a struggle for its control, on the principle that half a loaf is better than none.

In all these circumstances, Japanese policy would adjust to ensure that Japan would not remain exposed or isolated. Fantastic as it may seem today, an adjustment would not necessarily preclude some rapprochement with the Soviet Union, whether with the objective of countering new threats from other quarters or whether to keep in step with the United States or China. The success of such a policy would depend on the variables in the bilateral relationship and on Soviet policies.

Since the main direction of Soviet economic strategy is towards Western Europe, there seems little prospect of rapprochement via the economic route, at least for the remainder of this decade, even though the Soviets might depend on economic cooperation with Japan in several key areas. However, there is an intriguing suggestion that once the BAM railway is completed some time in the mid-1980s, the Soviet Union might again become very interested in the economic development of eastern Siberia and seek Japanese and US cooperation to recover the huge capital investment in the construction of the second Siberian railway.[25] This might lead in turn to a more conciliatory attitude, including a softening of the Soviet stand over the territorial issue.

Such Soviet overtures might coincide with a new disillusionment in

Japan with the prospect of substantial supplies of raw materials, especially coal and oil, from China by the end of the decade, which would increase Japanese interest in the development of Soviet east Asia. It would, of course, be much more difficult for the Japanese to modify their demands for the return of all four of the Northern Territories.

The Soviets would be largely responsible if any attempt to improve relations foundered on this issue. Their intransigence and the attempt to link the return of any of the islands to a fundamental change in Japanese foreign policy, i.e. the abandonment of the association with the United States, have had the effect of hardening the Japanese position. The Soviets apparently subscribe to the mistaken belief that Japan only understands and responds to policies of threat and force. This may be true in the short run, but they need only think back to the Triple Intervention in 1895, when Russia joined Germany and France in 'advising' Japan to disgorge the Liaodong peninsula, which it had acquired by the treaty of Shimonoseki at the end of the Sino–Japanese War. Ten years later Russia was to pay dearly for arousing Japan's enmity. Attempts to bully Japan only serve to strengthen its determination.

Behind the Soviet Union's approach to Japan lies a fear born out of historical experience and a Marxist interpretation of current events. Marxist analysis suggests that Japan has embarked on a new drive to dominate east Asia. Its rulers

have learned the lessons of the last war; economic infirmity, which the Japanese imperialists offset by military force, was one of the outstanding reasons for the failure of Japan's plans for expansion. To eliminate this shortcoming and create a durable economic base with technologically advanced industry and a corresponding level of military might – such are the compelling ambitions of Japanese monopolies.[26]

The argument continues that, although US power and influence are declining, Japan is prepared to continue with the mutual security treaty for a while in order to wring concessions from the Americans before the inevitably severe conflict between the two imperialist powers erupts. The big prize is a new association with China. To achieve that end, the forces of bourgeois nationalism in China must be encouraged and the Sino–Soviet conflict fostered to open the way for Japanese penetration of China.

The great fear that haunts the Soviets is the formation of a Sino–Japanese 'alliance', more threatening than the existing American–Japanese 'alliance'. The contradictions between Japan and the United States will eventually undermine the mutual security treaty. A Sino–Japanese bloc, on the other hand, conjures up visions of an aggressive union cemented by 'racist-nationalism'. Soviet writers have accused Mao of having deviated from the universal class struggle to pursue a 'racist-nationalist' struggle which coincides with the objectives of the Japanese 'reactionaries'. Mao's successors have shown little sign so far of changing course. On the contrary, they seem intent on opening China to Japanese economic penetration.

It is ironic that Soviet policies are a major influence in driving Japan into China's arms. The rigidity over the territorial dispute – in contrast to China's flexibility over the Senkaku islands – the downgrading of eastern Siberian development in favour of development in western Siberia, the frequent lapses in handling Japanese sensibilities and the emphasis on Soviet military might have the cumulative effect of making the Soviet Union a formidable and forbidding neighbour. China's economic potential is enormous, but that is not the only reason for Japanese interest in its development. Given the many problems and uncertainties surrounding China's ambitious modernization plan, the Japanese government periodically tries to revive the flagging enthusiasm of Japanese enterprises with special inducements. Its objective is both economic and strategic: to ensure Japan's leading role in China's modernization and to build it up as a counterweight to the Soviet Union.[27]

However, the long-term effect of such a policy may bring about the fate of the sorcerer's apprentice. A truly modernized China would become the dominant power in the region and, far from dancing to Japan's tune, may eventually make Japan dance to its tune. That is a prospect for the twenty-first century and Japanese politicians are not given to far-sighted calculations. But if such a prospect became more likely, then Japan's flexible approach to international politics might lead to an attempt to balance the influence of the new China by mending fences with the Soviet Union.

Two contradictory theses are usually advanced in discussions about Japan's future relations with China: either that they will become increasingly intimate and lead to the formation of a Sino–Japanese bloc, or that they are doomed to enter upon a collision course in the struggle for domination over east Asia. The former is perhaps the more widely held and it rests on the powerful argument that the two peoples are mutually attracted through their cultural and ethnic kinship. Certainly, many Japanese talk in those terms. In contrast, Russians and Americans will always remain outsiders. That may be so, but, quite apart from the impact of the unpredictable development of global economics and politics, the Japanese and Chinese will have to modify their pride and exclusiveness considerably before such an osmosis can come about.

In contrast to the mutual perceptions of Japanese and Chinese, the mutual perceptions of Japanese and Russians are often explained as the consequence of mutual racial antagonism. The Russians may have some gut feeling about the 'Yellow Peril', but their ideology refuses to acknowledge it. The idea that the Japanese are implacably hostile to Russia on racial grounds is unconvincing, although they are among the most racially and culturally self-conscious people in the world. Racial antipathy can play an important part in international politics, but it is not a constant of such politics. For instance, there was a time when racialism played a major part in American–Japanese relations, but the experience since 1945 has shown that it is not a permanent feature of the relationship.

The ultimate determinant in Soviet–Japanese relations, however, is the Soviet perception of security. Given their obsession with security and their gloomy analysis of the dynamics of international politics, there seems little prospect that the Soviets will come to regard Japan as a friendly and harmless neighbour, except on their own terms, i.e. a neutralist and lightly armed Japan without formal ties to any other major power and perhaps having the kind of relations with the Soviet Union that Finland has. Only under such circumstances might they be prepared to make some territorial concessions.

Neutrality or non-alignment has some attraction for the Japanese, but it would be unacceptable if it could be construed in any way as a surrender to Soviet pressure. Moreover, Japan is caught in a paradox from which there seems to be no escape at present. It requires the close association with the United States in order not to feel directly threatened by the Soviet Union, but that association severely limits the room for manoeuvre in efforts to improve the bilateral relationship with its northern neighbour.

Appendix: The dispute over the Northern Territories
The four Northern Territories in question are a small group of islands known as the Habomais; a larger island, Shikotan, lying off the Nemuro Peninsula of Hokkaido, which the Japanese regard as an extension of that island and the Soviets call the 'Little Kuriles', and the two southernmost islands of the Kurile chain, Kunashiri and Etorofu (Kunashir and Iturup in Russian). The islands have a combined land area of about 5,000 square kilometres (more than twice that of Okinawa prefecture) and had a population of about 17,000 Japanese inhabitants at the end of the Second World War. About half fled immediately at the time of the Soviet occupation; the remainder were interned and later forcibly repatriated between 1947 and 1949, so that no Japanese live on the islands today.

The history of the Japanese–Russian encounter in this region is very complex.[28] Both countries dispute the right to ownership of the Kuriles on historical grounds, although the Japanese claim that the Northern Territories and all the Kurile islands were included in a map of Japan in 1694, nearly a century before the Russians made their first appearance in the Kuriles. In negotiations preceding the treaty of commerce, navigation and delimitation, signed at Shimoda in 1855, the Russians laid claim to Etorofu but not the other islands which are now in dispute. By the terms of the treaty all four Northern Territories were recognized as Japanese and the islands north of Etorofu as Russian. The island of Sakhalin was to remain open to settlement by both Japanese and Russians, without national boundaries.

In 1875, by the treaty of St Petersburg, the Japanese acquired the rest of the Kurile chain northwards to Kamchatka peninsula in return for ceding their rights in Sakhalin. They took southern Sakhalin in 1905 by the treaty of Portsmouth which ended the Russo–Japanese War.

At Yalta, in February 1945, Roosevelt agreed that southern Sakhalin and the Kuriles should pass to the Soviet Union in return for a promise to enter the war against Japan after Germany's surrender. Moreover, he appeared to be under the erroneous impression that the Kuriles had been taken from the Soviets at the end of the 1904–5 war.

The Soviets occupied southern Sakhalin, Etorofu, Kunashiri, the Habomais and Shikotan at the end of the war and incorporated Sakhalin and the Kuriles into the Soviet Union. It is suggested that they occupied the Habomais and Shikotan as a result of a procedural error. Although the Japanese military units stationed there during the war were under the Chishima (Kurile) command, these islands belonged to and were under the administration of Hokkaido prefecture. In August 1945 the imperial headquarters ordered units on the Kuriles to surrender to the Soviets and units in Hokkaido to surrender to the Americans. Those on the Habomais and Shikotan thus surrendered to the Soviets by mistake.

In Chapter II, Article 2(c) of the treaty of San Francisco, Japan renounced all rights and claims to southern Sakhalin and the Kuriles but the treaty did not specify to whom they were to belong. One reason why the Soviets refused to sign the treaty was that their rights to sovereignty over the Kuriles were not specifically recognized. The Japanese, for their part, interpreted 'The Kuriles' mentioned in Article 2 as meaning the same islands as those mentioned in Article 2 of the treaty of St Petersburg, i.e. the islands north of Etorofu. Matters were made worse for the Russians by the provision of Article 25 that 'For the purposes of the present Treaty the Allied Powers shall be the States at war with Japan . . . provided that in each case the State concerned has signed and ratified the Treaty'. It went on to declare: 'nor shall any right, title or interest of Japan be deemed to be diminished or prejudiced by any provision of the Treaty in favour of a State which is not an Allied Power as so defined'.

The joint declaration of 1956, which reestablished diplomatic relations between the Soviet Union and Japan, stipulated in Article 9 that the Habomais and Shikotan should be returned to Japan on conclusion of a peace treaty between the two countries, but made no mention of the other territories. It had seemed as if the Japanese government would be content to settle for the islands off Nemuro, but pressures within the LDP, arising from the exigencies of factional politics, and a US intervention during the course of the Japanese–Soviet negotiations, made it harden its position to include claims to Etorofu and Kunashiri. Since the Japanese changed their position in the middle of negotiations, there was no prospect of signing the hoped-for peace treaty, which had been the original intention.

Ever since 1956 the argument has turned on the interpretation of the Allied wartime agreements, the San Francisco treaty and the declaration of 1956. In 1960 the Soviets added the stipulation that no territories would be returned until all US troops had been withdrawn from Japan. The debate remains somewhat inconclusive as not all the relevant Japanese documents of the immediate post-war years have been declassified.

So far, the issue seems insoluble as the Japanese insist on the return of all four territories, while the Soviet Union oscillates between refusal to consider any claim and hints that it might be prepared to negotiate over the Habomais and Shikotan. The Japanese, however, maintain that the Soviets are committed to recognizing the existence of a dispute by the terms of the communiqué signed at the conclusion of Prime Minister Tanaka's visit to Moscow in October 1973. In it both sides agreed that a peace treaty depended on 'resolving the yet unresolved problems since World War II'. Mr Tanaka claims that he received an oral assurance from President Brezhnev that the Northern Territories issue was included in the phrase 'the yet unresolved problems'.

The territories have considerable strategic importance and are situated in major fishing grounds.

Notes

[1]   On 6 September 1976, a Soviet pilot landed his MiG–25 (Foxbat) fighter at Hakodate in Hokkaido and sought political asylum in the United States. The pilot was allowed to proceed to the United States amidst Soviet accusations that he had been 'prevented' from returning home. The plane was dismantled and transferred to a Self-Defence Forces base to be inspected by Japanese and US experts. It was returned to the Soviet Union by freighter more than two months later and after much haggling between Japan and the Soviet Union. See *Defense of Japan 1977* (Tokyo, Defense Agency, 1977), ch. 4.

[2] Joint Declaration by the Union of Soviet Socialist Republics and Japan, signed in Moscow, 19 October 1956 (*United Nations: Treaty Series*, vol. 263 (1957), pp. 112–16).

[3] George A. Lensen, *Japanese Recognition of the USSR: Soviet–Japanese Relations 1921–1930* (Tokyo, Sophia University, 1970), pp. 8–9, 129–31.

[4] *Japan Times Weekly*, 15 August 1981.

[5] *International Herald Tribune*, 13/14 February 1982.

[6] *Technology and Soviet Energy Availability* (Washington, DC, Office of Technology Assessment, November 1981), ch. 2, 'Japanese–Soviet energy relations', p. 325.

[7] The Soviets threatened to cancel a tentative agreement to import 300,000 tonnes of steel plates unless the Japanese companies reduced the interest rate from 7.75 to 7.25 per cent or less for the five-year period covered by the credit. They warned that they would turn to European suppliers (Austria was reported to have offered a 7 per cent interest rate, while France, West Germany, Italy and the Netherlands had offered 7.25 per cent). In the end, agreement was reached after MITI had fixed interest at 7.25 per cent. See *Neue Zürcher Zeitung*, 10 September 1981. The Soviets have also pointed out that Japan's support for economic sanctions has cost it orders which were taken up by French and West German firms. N. Nikolayev and A. Pavlov, 'USSR–Japan: the goodneighbourliness course and its enemies', *International Affairs* (Moscow), no. 8 (August 1982), p. 35.

[8] *Technology and Soviet Energy Availability*, ch. 2, p. 325.

[9] Tony Scanlon, 'Outlook for Soviet oil', *Science*, vol. 217 (23 July 1982), pp. 325–30.

[10] This problem is discussed in Wolf Mendl, *Issues in Japan's China Policy* (London, Macmillan for the RIIA, 1978), pp. 88–9.

[11] *Asian Security 1981* (Tokyo, Research Institute for Peace and Security, 1981), p. 80.

[12] *Defense of Japan 1982* (Tokyo, Defense Agency, 1982).

[13] Speech by Yoshio Sakurauchi on 3 September 1981; see *Japan Times*, 4 September 1981.

[14] On 18 January 1980 the police arrested a retired major-general of the Ground Self-Defence Forces and two junior officers on charges of passing military secrets to the Soviet embassy.

[15] The *Admiral Nakhimov* was a cruiser of the Imperial Russian Navy and was sunk off Tsushima in 1905. In 1980 a millionaire, Ryoichi Sasakawa, financed salvage operations in order to retrieve its reported cargo of gold and other treasures. The Japanese government laid claim to the wreck on the grounds that it had been captured on 28 May 1905, and the Japanese flag was raised to declare proprietary rights. The Soviets lodged a counter-claim, denying that it had been captured by the Japanese. Sasakawa added insult to injury by offering to return the treasure to the Soviet Union in exchange for the Northern Territories. Tempers rose during an exchange between the Soviet ambassador and a Foreign Ministry official on 31 October 1980. Ambassador Polyansky described the salvage operations as 'basically not very different from an act of piracy'. The man from the Gaimusho retorted that such

a suggestion was 'an affront to the feelings of the Japanese people'. See *Japan Times Weekly*, 25 October and 1 November 1980; and *Japan* (London, Information Centre of the Japanese Embassy), no. 121 (5 November 1980).

[16] *Japan*, no. 138 (18 March 1981); *Frankfurter Allgemeine Zeitung*, 18 March 1981; Hiroshi Kimura, 'Wie ist der Wechsel des sowjetischen Botschafters in Japan zu bewerten?', translated from *Sankei Shimbun*, 25 January 1982, in Joachim Glaubitz, *Materialien zur Aussen- und Sicherheitspolitik Japans*, Folge 1982/1 (Ebenhausen, Stiftung Wissenschaft und Politik, April 1982), pp. 4–8.

[17] *Japan Times*, 28 April and 3 and 23 May 1981.

[18] Between 1945 and 1980 the Soviets seized 1,616 Japanese fishing vessels and interned 13,257 crew members. Some 1,001 vessels were eventually returned, 25 sank due to accidents and 590 were still in custody. Of the fishermen, 37 died in prison, 13,218 were repatriated and 2 were still held in 1980. See Toru Nakagawa, 'Why the Northern Territories belong to Japan', *Japan Echo*, vol. 8, no. 3 (Autumn 1981), p. 85.

[19] Being 'friendly' has included the passing on of information about the SDF, the police and anti-Soviet activities; offers of cameras, cassette recorders and photocopying machines. The 'privileges' are the right to fish in restricted Soviet territorial waters.

[20] *Straits Times*, 23 January 1981; and *Neue Zürcher Zeitung*, 8/9 February 1981.

[21] *Japan Echo*, vol. 8, no. 3 (Autumn 1981), p. 77.

[22] *Soviet News* (London, Embassy of the Soviet Union), 30 March 1982.

[23] *Japan Times Weekly*, 17 and 24 April, 1 May 1982.

[24] For some time all the opposition parties, with the exception of the Japan Communist Party and the pro-Soviet element in the Socialist Party, have accepted the Mutual Security Treaty system in varying degrees. This became clear from the party platforms adopted during the election campaign in June 1980. See *Japan Times Weekly*, 14 and 21 June 1980; *Japan*, no. 109 (30 July 1980). Public opinion polls, too, have continued to reveal substantial majorities in its favour as against those who are opposed to it. See *Japan Echo*, vol. 8, no. 3 (Autumn 1981), p. 49; *Japan*, no. 166 (19 November 1981).

[25] *Asian Security 1981*, pp. 39–40.

[26] N. I. Sladkovsky, *China and Japan: Past and Present* (originally published in Moscow in 1971), edited and translated by Robert F. Price (Gulf Breeze, Fla, Academic International Press, 1975), pp. 249–50.

[27] For a discussion of the economic relationship between Japan and China, see Wolf Mendl, 'Japan and China: the economic nexus', in the forthcoming volume Nobutoshi Akao (ed.), *Japan's Economic Security* (London, Gower for RIIA, 1983).

[28] The most comprehensive treatment of the whole issue is to be found in John J. Stephan, *The Kurile Islands: Russo–Japanese Frontier in the Pacific* (Oxford, Clarendon Press, 1974). Other sources include Wolf Mendl, *Issues in Japan's China Policy*, pp. 79–80, note 31; *Japan Times Weekly*, 21 January 1978; Toru Nakagawa, 'Why the Northern Territories belong to Japan'; and *Japan*, no. 200 (26 August 1982).

6 The Soviet Union and Korea
Gerald Segal

The Soviet Union's smallest frontier is the 10.4 mile boundary with the Democratic People's Republic of Korea (DPRK).[1] While one does not wish to suggest that geopolitics is the source of all wise political judgements, the tiny frontier does match Moscow's relative disregard of Korea. The marshland on the Soviet side of the boundary, formed by the lower course of the Tumen river, is also symbolic of the Soviet Union's uncertain footing in its relations with Korea since 1945 and the predicaments of power that have encouraged the Soviets to minimize the importance of Korea in their foreign policy.

Staying with our geographic theme, it is important to note that Korea's strategic position at the crossroads of east Asian politics has earned it the title of 'the Palestine of east Asia'.[2] Korea had long been a prime example of a homogeneous nation-state, but was also a focus of great-power concern not because of its intrinsic value, but more because it was on a road to China, Japan or Manchuria. From an early date the Koreans learnt how to play off foreign powers against each other, but inevitably Korea has also been a place where complex webs of international politics were often woven. In terms of Soviet foreign policy, the original interest in Korea can be traced to the 1860 Sino-Russian treaty of Peking, delimiting the Tumen border, and the 1895 treaty of Shimonoseki which marked the establishment of Russian power and China's decline.[3] The 1905 treaty of Portsmouth signalled the limits of Russian power and the rise of Japan, but the 1945 defeat of Japanese forces by the Soviet Union and the agreement with the United States to temporarily split the Korean peninsula heralded yet another change in the great-power fortunes at this Korean crossroads. What is more, this historical pattern highlights the importance of three states in any analysis of Soviet involvement in Korea: China, Japan and the United States.

Consequently, this essay will focus not on Soviet–Korean relations as such, but rather on the way in which Korean issues have featured in

Sino–Soviet, Soviet–American and Soviet–Japanese relations. The adoption of this great-power approach does not mean that the Koreans are seen as marionettes on other people's strings. On the contrary, the centrality of Korean concern with *chuche* (self-identity or self-reliance)[4] has meant that great powers have found it very difficult to control the Koreans. The parallel to that other crossroads, in Palestine, illustrates the predicaments of great powers when negotiating over the bodies of fiercely independent local states.

Before proceeding to the main analysis, a word should be said about the strength of Soviet interest in Korea. The extension of Russian/ Soviet power to Korea is relatively recent and Moscow continues to be seen as an outsider. Soviet power in its own far eastern territories is also relatively new and while large investments are now being made in Siberian industry and a second railway line to the east, direct Soviet involvement in east Asia is a new phenomenon.[5]

The Soviet Union's specific bilateral links to Korea remain of slight importance to Moscow. To begin with, there is no large ethnic Korean population in the USSR, even in border areas. Some North Koreans are sent to work in east Asian Siberia, but the numbers remain small. Soviet–Korean trade remains less than 1 per cent of the entire Soviet total (30 per cent of DPRK trade) and recent Soviet commentaries speak frankly of further trade problems caused by the DPRK's failure to fulfil contracts.[6]

Unlike the Soviet Union's western frontiers, there are few strong links to local politics and therefore the Soviet Union's relative unconcern with Korea should not be surprising. However, there undoubtedly have been important Soviet interactions with its larger rivals in the east over Korea, and therefore Soviet–American relations are a good place to begin the analysis.

Superpower predicaments

The Soviet Union's lightning campaign in Manchuria and Korea in 1945 left Moscow's troops in control of nearly all the Korean peninsula. A month later, when the first US troops arrived, the Red Army voluntarily withdrew to a line arbitrarily drawn by the United States and accepted by the Soviets, at the 38th parallel.[7] Soviet involvement in Korea, as in Eastern Europe, was achieved with US connivance. Superpower agreements, combined with simultaneous rivalry, led to the first and most obvious of the USSR's predicaments of power: should US power and presence in Korea be vigorously opposed? On the one hand Washington's presence was licensed by the same law as Moscow's presence. On the other hand, an absent United States would give the Soviet Union more leeway.

The licence to power in Korea for the Soviet Union also meant it could bring along its friends. The soon to be installed DPRK strong-man, Kim Il-sung, entered Korea in a Soviet military uniform and by 1948 had assumed full control by purging much of his Chinese-supported opposition.[8] However, Kim's clothing is insufficient reason for blaming the Soviet Union for starting the June 1950 Korean War. The causes of that war have been debated elsewhere, but for the purposes of this chapter it is sufficient to suggest that Kim may well have jumped the starting gun primed by an opportunistic Stalin.[9] This predicament of a superpower unable to control an independently minded ally was to become increasingly evident elsewhere in post-war crisis management.

The Korean War also illustrated the difficulty of calculating risk in conflict involving the other superpower. Kim Il-sung's leap before the starting gun may have been forgotten by Moscow if he had been swiftly successful in the war. However, the DPRK's stalled military operation unfortunately presented the Soviets with the uncomfortable need to manage superpower crises in an area considered peripheral by Stalin.[10] Potential German rearmament, US power in Europe and NATO were all issues of far greater importance to the Soviets, and ones which all took a turn for the worse when the Korean War spurred West Euro-peans to close ranks even more closely with the United States. No solution has yet been found to the predicament of a global power trying to reconcile divergent regional objectives.

The best that Stalin could then hope for was a controlled crisis in Korea. The Chinese eventually sent their troops into combat across the Yalu river, but the Soviet Union never crossed the Tumen. Soviet commentaries would later claim that they offered Kim crucial military aid,[11] but the reality was more in keeping with Moscow's attempt to keep out of a direct clash with US troops. Soviet pilots never flew over territory not held by DPRK troops and the Soviet navy never interfered with US naval operations in the Sea of Japan. Moscow apparently ran the coordinated communist operations from a Manchurian base, but officially it was solely a Sino–Korean effort. Soviet aircraft only fired on US patrols in September 1950 when the United States strafed a Man-churian airfield. The accidental US air strike on 8 October on a Soviet airfield 18 miles from Vladivostok provoked nothing but a nasty Soviet protest note. Only after Chinese forces pushed the United States to a stalemate midway along the Korean peninsula and the war stabilized, did the Soviet Union introduce 25,000 troops in defensive operations, including 5,000 artillery and 7,500 anti-aircraft troops. In November 1952 the United States shot down a Soviet aircraft, but neither side publicized the event because the plane was based out of Vladivostok. To have made an issue of these or any other incidents would have been to court an open superpower crisis.[12]

From the Soviet Union's point of view as a superpower, the Korean War was a well-managed crisis. Sino–Soviet and Soviet–Korean relations (see next section) were strained in the course of the combat,[13] but Washington and Moscow avoided a direct clash in this still formative and dangerous period of the Cold War. When the Korean War ground to a halt, the Soviet Union's attention shifted swiftly back to Europe. Moscow's main interest in Korea seemed to begin and end with Stalin. It was one of the many predicaments of power which led the Soviets to conclude that local north-east Asian tensions did not always serve global superpower objectives. But Moscow's neglect of the DPRK in 1950 in the end resulted in a more independent Pyongyang, and hence sowed the seeds of future problems.

By the late 1960s the Soviet Union was more concerned with a rival China than with a rival United States in the region. The shift in Soviet priorities was most evident in the formulation of Brezhnev's 1969 Asian Collective Security scheme. This attempt to build a containment wall around China in Asia involved Korea in the Sino–Soviet conflict and still meant that Soviet–US relations over Korea remained of lesser importance.[14] But locally initiated crises could bring the superpowers back into confrontation in Korea.

The first of three superpower crises began on 23 January 1968 when DPRK forces seized the US intelligence ship, *Pueblo*. The Soviet predicament was essentially how much support it should give Kim Il-sung. Not to aid Kim would be to lose DPRK support, assist China and miss an opportunity of embarrassing the United States. On the other hand, to play down the crisis would be to assist nascent superpower détente and avoid needless tension in a dangerous superpower crisis. As with previous examples of unwanted Asian crisis (e.g. over the Taiwan straits) Moscow chose to offer low-key support to Korea while keeping the Soviet Union out of direct involvement. The related predicament for Soviet national security – whether to defend Vladivostok with a high- or low-profile response – was also resolved by an attempt to minimize the danger.

When the United States responded to the DPRK piracy by assembling the largest naval task force since the Cuban missile crisis, Moscow reacted with only as much firmness as was required to deter US punishment of Korea, but not enough to raise the crisis fever.[15] No authoritative Soviet commentary on the crisis was issued until after the US–DPRK talks began at Panmunjom and then the *Observer* of 4 February declared support only from the 'socialist community'. As in the 1958 Taiwan straits crisis, Soviet support for its ally came only after tension was being reduced. What is more, in response to the presence of the US task force the Soviets used a much smaller capability, and it was brought into play only after the United States announced it was withdrawing the main spearhead of the force in early February. Only then did *Red Star* mention for the first time the 1961 Soviet–Korean defence treaty. The 9–10 February visit by Boris Ponomarev to Pyongyang apparently resulted in more arms sales, but not even of the quality then being supplied to Egypt.

But neither could the Soviet Union be seen to serve US interests. US requests for Soviet 'good offices' in contacting Pyongyang were repeatedly refused, for as in the Vietnam War negotiations, Moscow could not be perceived as urging 'capitulation' of its allies.[16] This predicament encouraged caution and a minimal Soviet reaction. The Soviet Union was most unlikely to have been involved in the original decision to seize the *Pueblo*, and seemed to be forced to make the best of a bad, locally initiated crisis.[17] The preeminent importance of global relations with the United States meant that the *Pueblo* crisis made the Soviet predicaments in Korea more acute.

The second DPRK-inspired crisis drew an even more restrained Soviet response. On 15 April 1969, DPRK fighters shot down a US EC–121 reconnaissance aircraft over the Sea of Japan. The new US administration responded with an even larger naval task force than was summoned for the *Pueblo* (including four aircraft carriers and three cruisers), but the Soviet Union acted even less forthrightly in Kim Il-sung's defence.[18] Moscow offered mild verbal support for Kim, but Soviet destroyers helped the US search for survivors and one ship sent a condolence message to a US craft involved in the search. Moscow seemed to resolve its predicaments of power to a certain extent by trying to ignore Korean provocation. The DPRK had supported the Soviet invasion of Czechoslovakia in 1968 but in general Soviet–Korean relations were cooling. Soviet–American détente was just getting back on track and therefore the Soviets were no doubt pleased that the EC–121 issue was not raised at the United Nations where they would have had to defend the DPRK more resolutely. On 15 May, during a visit to Pyongyang, President Podgorny rebuked North Korea for its rash action and the critical sections of his speech were omitted by the DPRK press.[19]

The only event that did draw a sharp Soviet note was the presence of the large US task force near Vladivostok. On 21 April a Soviet diplomatic message made it plain that apart from the threat the task force posed to Moscow's security interests, no issue should get in the way of Soviet global policy. It seemed that the Soviet Union was beginning to resolve some of its predicaments and priorities regarding superpower relations in Korea. US presence was increasingly tolerated as long as Soviet security was safeguarded. The détente era eased some predicaments of power for both superpowers.

The third Korean crisis reinforced this trend. On 18 August 1976 two US soldiers were axed to death by DPRK soldiers in the demilitarized zone. Washington responded by forming a small naval task force and alerting various troops in the area.[20] The Soviet response this time was limited to a mild verbal rebuke with no additional military movement. Apparently the Kremlin was getting fed up with DPRK provocations, especially when Moscow was unable to strengthen seriously its own ambivalent status in Pyongyang. The Soviet Union's recognition of Kim Il-sung's independence seemed to lessen many of its superpower predicaments, especially when détente with the United States seemed to be bearing fruit.

The détente era did not however resolve another Soviet problem regarding Korea. Moscow's ambivalent attitude towards the reunification of Korea, especially in the 1970s, was put under a great deal of strain. In the 1970s there were several reports of Soviet contacts with representatives of the Republic of Korea (ROK), but none amounted to official recognition.[21] The Soviets encouraged Kim Il-sung's détente offensive in the same decade in the hope that the local states would get the Soviet Union out of the predicament in which they had placed them in the first place.[22] Unfortunately for Moscow, the Korean stalemate was not broken.

The Soviet Union's dilemma over the issue of reunification bears some resemblances to those faced by the Soviet Union in Europe. The United States as the guarantor power for a divided Germany and a divided Korea is thousands of miles away with only a garrison of troops set up as a 'trip-wire' to deter forced unification. In the German case, unification is on balance unacceptable to the Soviets for fear of creating an additional European power. In Korea, unification poses a different problem in that it might result in a Chinese gain (see next section), and if achieved violently might lead to a serious crisis with Washington. So it should not be surprising to see the Soviet Union firmly supporting a peaceful unification of Korea, but not pressing too hard even for this minimal objective.[23] The removal of US power from Korea that would follow unification would probably be in the Soviet interest, but not if it meant a united Korea under Chinese or Japanese dominance. The stakes are high, therefore providing strong reason for living with the predicaments of power. It seems clear that the greatest problems for superpower relations in Korea arise from an unstable local situation, whether it be in DPRK initiatives or the ROK's tenuous grip on power. If the superpowers have learnt anything about Korea in 35 years, it is the primacy of these local factors.

Sino–Soviet predicaments

Sino–Soviet relations regarding Korea are simpler for the Soviet Union to manage than the superpower relations already discussed. Essentially the problem has been to what extent China's involvement in Korean affairs should be vigorously opposed. No clear-cut solution is apparent.

Chinese involvement in Korea predates that of the Soviet Union, and even before Soviet troops occupied northern Korea, Chinese and Soviet factions were fighting for the leadership of the Korean Communist Party. While it would be an error to 'read back' deep conflict when none existed during the Sino–Soviet honeymoon, it is important to state that tension between the communist giants over Korea has deep roots.[24] These problems were outweighed at the time by the need to unite against a common enemy and establish the DPRK. Thus tension and cooperation coexisted, with no one, including Stalin, judging it worth risking the revolution for the sake of partisan interests.

The same pattern is evident during the Korean War itself. The use of Chinese troops across the Yalu was clearly in the Soviet interest as it helped prop up Kim Il-sung. The predicament for Moscow was how much it should help build up Chinese influence in Korea by supporting the Chinese military operation. In the end the Soviets seemed to opt for a 'short-tether' policy, whether by choice or because of lack of political and economic resources.[25] The Soviet Union was a contributory rather than a decisive factor in the Chinese decision to intervene, and Moscow was well aware of the secret pact between the Chinese and Korean communist parties, signed in Moscow in 1949 and providing for mutual security. (No similar treaty was signed between Kim and the Soviet Union.)[26] But while Stalin lived, and Sino–Soviet relations were relatively close, Beijing's relative independence was not a problem for Moscow. China and Korea lacked any alternative option during the war and so they relied on Soviet support and made do with the equipment provided. Official Soviet accounts of the war minimized China's role, but in the essential crisis management China and the United States were squared off while Moscow protected its own national security.[27] As the war wound down the Soviet attention shifted back to Europe, Sino–Korean relations emerged from the war much warmer than Soviet–Korean ties. However, as all were members of the same bloc, this seemed a price worth paying for the Soviet Union's broader foreign policy objectives.

The problems became more acute for the Soviet leadership with the onset of de-Stalinization by Khrushchev. The Stalin question in Pyongyang, as in Beijing, deepened policy cleavages and in the DPRK the Soviet ambassador was implicated in convoluted Korean factional struggles against Kim Il-sung.[28] As the Sino–Soviet split deepened, Korea seemed to be just a few paces behind China in opposing what was becoming known as 'revisionism'. China's contentious Great Leap Forward was matched by Korea's Flying Horse Movement, and Beijing's opposition to 'peaceful coexistence' with the United States found sympathy in Pyongyang. China, like Korea, had irredentist claims against a US-supported state. This, coupled with joint dissatisfaction with the Soviet model and irritation at the Soviet Union's meddling in domestic politics, meant that it was only natural for Moscow to lose the first stages of competition with China over Korea.[29]

Soviet–Korean relations in the late 1950s and early 1960s were not completely gloomy. While it would be convenient to attribute the rises and falls in Moscow–Pyongyang ties to a determined Soviet policy, in fact it seemed to be merely a reflection of the general fluctuating nature of Sino–Soviet relations. Khrushchev was unwilling to make special concessions to win Kim Il-sung's favour, for when Moscow and Beijing signed defence pacts with the DPRK in 1961 only the Sino–Korean one was of unlimited duration and did not mention the UN Charter.[30] In the early 1960s Korea supported China in its clash with India, backed Albania in the polemics with the Soviet Union and was soon criticizing 'revisionism' nearly as firmly as was Beijing.

In 1963 Soviet economic and military aid to the DPRK was severed and, although the two states refrained from open polemics, the split was evident. Under Khrushchev, the Soviets had finally decided to sidestep the predicament of competing with China for Korean favours. The result was that Beijing won the first round and Moscow lost its Korean ally. In later years, this period was to be ignored in Soviet analyses, for it was apparently one of defeat and lacking imaginative policy.[31]

The issue was revived when Khrushchev was ousted in October 1964 and the new Soviet leadership tried to woo back both Beijing and Pyongyang. Unfortunately there were no simple answers to the predicaments of power. Much as in the case of Soviet attempts to win Chinese and Vietnamese friendship in late 1964/early 1965, Moscow sent envoys to the DPRK. On his way back from Hanoi where he promised increased aid against the United States, Premier Kosygin stopped in Pyongyang and made similar promises. To be sure, the DPRK needed the assistance, but it was not in such desperate need that it would send them dashing back into Soviet arms. Soviet–Korean relations improved but, at least at first, this was not achieved at the expense of Sino–Korean ties.[32]

Indeed the Soviet Union probably hoped that better relations with the Asian communists would include China so that they could all engage in 'united action' against the United States in Vietnam. Moscow hoped to overcome its predicament by improving relations with China in the new mood of anti-Americanism of the Vietnam War. Unfortunately China's own strategic debate on 'united action' decided against cooperation with the Soviet Union while Korea and Vietnam saw good reason to stay united against the United States. Moscow's predicament on 'united action' in Vietnam remained,[33] but the Soviet Union made some progress in improving relations with Korea. China then proceeded to make matters easier for the Soviets (and harder for the DPRK) by making territorial claims against Korea and having Red Guards denounce Kim Il-sung as 'fat Kim'.[34] Nevertheless, Pyongyang still tried to balance its position by denouncing Soviet 'revisionism', while at the same time attending the CPSU Congress in Moscow in March 1966. The latter event was crucial as China's refusal to attend – thereby severing Party-to-Party ties with the Soviets – was a major landmark in the Sino–Soviet split.

The Soviet Union seemed resigned to the need to maintain proper ties with Korea, even if it could not entirely eliminate Chinese influence. Unlike Khrushchev, the new Soviet leadership seemed prepared to live with the ambiguities of aid, but little influence, while enduring some hostile criticism. This basic predicament of 'superpower–client' relationships was becoming increasingly well known to Moscow in Asia, if only because of Soviet–Vietnamese ties. This trend was once again visible during the *Pueblo* crisis when, despite meagre Chinese support, Moscow could gain no satisfaction from the limited risks it took on Pyongyang's behalf. The Soviets had the problem of keeping China at bay, but no satisfaction of having improved relations with the DPRK in return. The EC–121 incident in fact revealed a weakening of the position as China attacked superpower collusion (i.e. Soviet aid in the sea search). In 1969 Korea refused to attend the preparatory meetings for Moscow's anti-China get-together of world communist parties and refused to support the Soviets in the recent border clashes with China. Moscow still felt a need to support Korea in part because of the hope for anti-China support, but none was forthcoming.[35] Under the circumstances, the Soviet Union's decision to live with Sino–Soviet predicaments in Korea seemed the wisest move.

The DPRK's ability to balance Beijing and Moscow improved with the emergence of China from the Cultural Revolution and Zhou Enlai's visit to Pyongyang in April 1970. From then on the two communist giants had ups and downs in relations with Korea, but neither seemed able to remove the other's influence and both seemed prepared to tolerate this unsatisfactory state of affairs. Moscow made some gains when Nixon visited China in February 1972 and Gromyko invited his DPRK counterpart to Moscow. But China increased its aid and trade with Korea dramatically in the mid-1970s, and in his major trip abroad in 1975 Kim Il-sung stopped in China and Romania but not the Soviet Union. In Beijing, China said the DPRK was the 'sole and legal sovereign state of the Korean nation' and thereby appeared as Kim's leading supporter at a time when Moscow was seeking support against China in its Asian Collective Security scheme. The DPRK's default on economic agreements in 1977 was partly a result of debts for oil owed to the Soviet Union, failure to fulfil barter trade agreements and declining Soviet–Korean trade.[36] The balance shifted back in the Soviet Union's favour in the later 1970s when Pyongyang apparently supported the radical Gang of Four after Mao's death in 1976 and was generally displeased with signs of Sino–American cooperation and China's domestic liberalization. In 1978 Kim Il-sung accepted the Order of Lenin awarded to him six years previously, and in May 1980 Kim met Brezhnev (as well as Hua Guofeng) in Belgrade. What is more, repeated rumours of hidden Chinese trade with the ROK damaged Beijing's relative standing in Pyongyang.[37]

The decline of East–West détente, especially after the invasion of Afghanistan and the failure of the DPRK's own détente in the peninsula, gave the Soviets some new support in Pyongyang, although they still ranked marginally behind Beijing. Kim Il-sung's support for Norodom Sihanouk of Kampuchea, declared opposition to the Vietnamese invasion of Kampuchea and frosty statements about Soviet intervention in Afghanistan all indicated China's superior position, but reports that the Soviet navy was now using the ice-free port of Najin showed a still strong Soviet presence. In December 1981 China's Premier Zhao Ziyang visited the DPRK and sharply denounced the United States for opposing reunification, and Pyongyang criticized both 'imperialism and dominationism'. In early 1982 the DPRK was said to be seeking new oil supplies so as to free itself from reliance on both China and the Soviet Union.[38] But in the previous ten years there was no substantial change in China's and the Soviet Union's balanced position in Pyongyang. Neither communist power could dislodge the other, and both seemed resigned to living with that predicament.

On the subject of Korean reunification, by the early 1980s it was clear that both China and the Soviet Union were taking roughly the same position[39] (although both would be quick to deny any such congruence). One Soviet commentary in 1980 even suggested that the ROK had taken a more moderate line on DPRK peace proposals precisely because Beijing had improved relations with the United States and thereby undercut Seoul's position. The 1979 ROK–DPRK talks were said to be 'clearly prompted by the rapid development of relations between the USA and China'.[40] The Soviet Union's key concern seemed to be not that there might be a Chinese role, so much as the possibility that Moscow would be excluded from a Camp-David-style summit on Korea. Thus both the Soviets and Chinese supported peaceful unification, but neither seemed to want to risk a sudden US withdrawal. Once again it seemed to be up to the local Korean states to break the stalemate as the great powers were caught in their predicaments of power.

Soviet–Japanese predicaments

Unlike the two sets of predicaments already discussed, for quite some time the role of Korea in Soviet–Japanese relations was relatively straightforward. The Soviet Union entered Korea in 1945 by defeating Japan and for some time after Tokyo was seen from Moscow in a very negative light. This hostile image was not entirely due to the wartime legacy, but rather the Soviet attitude towards Japan was strongly influenced by the Soviet Union's struggle with the United States and its allies in Japan. Whatever the cause, Japan was still seen as an enemy, and so much so that it could serve as a main pretext for the 1950 Sino–Soviet friendship act and for keeping Korean communists in line.

Although it was not appreciated at the time, the Korean War planted the seeds of the Soviet Union's first dilemma regarding Japan. The invasion of the ROK spurred Western unity, including Japanese friendship with the United States, in an anti-communist coalition. Moscow apparently failed to realize that Korea was seen as a dagger pointing at Japan and tension on the peninsula sent Tokyo scuttling to the United States for protection, much as the West European allies responded to the increased Soviet threat in Europe. The Kremlin seemed to see Japan as having no legitimate interest in Korea and used hostility to Tokyo as a symbol to forge unity among east Asian communist parties.[41]

The real problems for Soviet policy arose when the Soviet Union sought to improve ties with Tokyo and undercut US influence there. The establishment of diplomatic relations between the Soviet Union and Japan in 1956 was the first major step along a road that was destined to be long and tortuous. Until the early 1970s Japan remained overwhelmingly a target for Soviet criticism and Tokyo clearly chose to deal with the ROK and to further their economic links,[42] despite the Japanese imperial legacy that made the establishment of its contacts in east Asia a delicate process.

Soviet–Japanese negotiations on economic cooperation, especially in the Soviet far east in the late 1960s, for the first time forced Moscow to confront difficult choices. Increased tension on the peninsula that was perceived either as a threat to Japan, or as something that might draw Japan into the conflict, made Tokyo less willing to deal with the Soviet Union. The *Pueblo* affair in particular concerned Moscow because at the time the Soviet Union was attempting to arrange major talks led by Suslov and Ponomarev in Japan. The crisis meant that the talks had to be postponed. The *Pueblo* itself had been based in Japan and so Tokyo was especially sensitive to how the crisis would be resolved.[43] As we have already seen, other pressures on the Soviet Union in Korea were pushing Moscow in a similar direction – that is to minimize the importance of Korea and controlling the DPRK.

Soviet–Japanese relations differed in one major way from broader superpower relations. During the détente of the 1970s Japan was apparently perceived as a less odious power than the United States and so both Pyongyang and Moscow made serious efforts to sew up major economic deals with Japan. For Pyongyang, Japan provided another lever to obtain independence from Beijing and Moscow, and in the mid-1970s Kim Il-sung embarked on major new foreign economic ventures with Japan. The Soviet Union was apparently not displeased with this effort, for Moscow was also pursuing contacts with Japan. There may also have been hopes that Japan could be wooed away from the United States.[44] Tokyo was fully prepared to 'separate politics from trade' but in the end these contacts were abruptly terminated. DPRK overspending and serious economic problems meant that ties to Japan had to be loosened. This, coupled with generally deteriorating East–West relations, made the opening to Japan short-lived.

Soviet–Japanese relations also cooled in the latter 1970s, but not for the same reasons. Moscow avoided a potential predicament of good Soviet–Japanese ties while contemporary Korean–Japanese ties were poor, but by accident not design. Soviet–Japanese problems came to a head in August 1978 when China and Japan signed a friendship pact. Moscow's attempts to keep China and Japan apart had failed and the Soviets in no small measure had themselves to blame. Japan had gained no significant concessions on the territorial issue with the Soviet Union, and continuing problems over Soviet military deployments and fishing eventually pushed Tokyo into Beijing's arms.[45] The damage to Soviet–Japanese relations was contained, but at the same time there was little prospect of improvement in bilateral ties. Moscow had hoped to include Japan, in one way or another, in its plans for an Asian Collective Security system directed against China, but Japan refused to be drawn into entangling alliances. The Soviets might have hoped at least to 'neutralize' Japan's growing power in east Asia, but the policy seemed to have failed by the end of the 1970s.[46] However, this problem for Soviet policy, as serious as it was, had more to do with Sino–Soviet–Japanese relations than Soviet–Korean–Japanese ties. At least on matters regarding Japan and North Korea, Moscow was in tune with Pyongyang, for a change. There have been few cases of Soviet–Japanese relations harming Soviet–Korean relations but that seems more fortuitous than the result of prescient planning. At its most basic level, the DPRK has now come to see Japan as a counterweight to its communist neighbours, and Moscow has reason to fear Japanese economic penetration of the region on that basis. A US withdrawal from South Korea that was simply replaced by Japan's presence would not be much improvement from a Soviet perspective.[47] More simply, in the Soviet view, Tokyo's ties to the ROK seem to fall conveniently into the category of an imperialist alliance to shore up the Seoul regime.[48] What has so far 'saved' Soviet–DPRK relations has been that the Soviet Union and Korea both wanted Japanese friendship in roughly the same period. This may not always be the case, and the Soviet predicament over ties to Japan may well return with greater force.

Conclusions: problems and predicaments

The process of 'proving' a negative proposition is always a suspect endeavour, but it should be clear from the above analysis that the Soviet Union does not have a strong intrinsic interest in Korea. Korean independence, the intractability of local issues and above all the conflicting priorities of power faced by the Soviet Union have all conspired to minimize the importance of Korean affairs for the Soviet Union. To the extent that the Soviets were concerned with Korea, it was primarily in the context of the three sets of bilateral relations: Soviet–American, Soviet–Chinese and Soviet–Japanese ties.

Overall, these three bilateral relationships provided a seven-fold division of the 35-year period from the beginning of Soviet occupation of Korea. (1) In 1945–50 the Soviet Union maintained virtual dominance of its part of Korea. (2) In 1950–3 the Soviets found themselves drawn into a dangerous crisis with the United States and henceforth became shy of involvement in further high tension in the area. (3) In 1954–8 the Soviets had a sort of honeymoon in Korea with simple animosity towards the United States and relative unity with the DPRK. (4) In 1959–64 the Soviet Union effectively lost control of the DPRK as the Sino–Soviet split led Moscow to withdraw to a great degree from active involvement in Korea. (5) In 1965–7 the Soviet Union returned to influence in the area but without much gusto. (6) In 1968–72 the Soviets seemed to accept that continuing predicaments with the United States, China and to a certain extent Japan could not be avoided. (7) From 1973 it was apparent to the Soviet Union that it was best to minimize the importance of Korean events as much as possible. There might be ups and downs in the various bilateral relations, but nothing much would be likely to change.

In this 35-year period it is apparent that the Soviet Union had four main objectives to pursue in relation to Korea. First, there was the normal desire to safeguard security against potential threats, whether they resulted from US intervention, Korean provocation or Chinese rivalry. Second was the desire to contain Chinese influence. This objective, although present before 1958, became particularly acute in the period between 1959 and 1972. The third objective of containing US influence used to be the second most important, but by the early 1960s, with signs of a thaw in East–West relations, containing China became more important. The fourth objective of containing Japanese influence is far less important than the previous three, and is now directed at the economic rather than the military potential of Japan. It should be clear that these four goals have been neither constant in importance nor mutually exclusive. Precisely because of these complications, it has been obvious that the Soviet Union faced certain basic predicaments in its attitude towards Korea. For example, an improvement in Sino–Soviet relations in Korea was unlikely to facilitate the best policy for superpower relations. As the Soviet proverb would have it, 'It is painful to sit on two chairs with one bottom'.[49]

Five predicaments of power stand out as being most painful to Soviet 'bottoms'. (1) Should the US presence be vigorously opposed? The withdrawal of the United States might further the cause of Korean nationalism but that might not necessarily be a positive development from the Soviet point of view. Soviet presence in Korea was sanctioned by similar great-power arguments and US withdrawal might only benefit Japan and China. (2) Should the Soviet Union become directly involved in crisis management? As a superpower the obvious answer should be yes, but Moscow has experienced the damage that can be done to its relations with the DPRK, the United States or China depending on the nature of Soviet involvement. The examples of Soviet crisis management in 1950–3, 1968, 1969 and 1976 are not some of Moscow's fondest memories. (3) Should the unification of Korea be pressed firmly? Unifying Korea with assurances of Soviet influence would of course be desirable. But such an outcome is far from certain, and rather than risk Chinese, Japanese or Korean challenges, the minimally important Korean peninsula is best left as it is. (4) Should the Chinese presence be vigorously opposed? This problem only became acute after the Sino–Soviet split, and Moscow seems to have discovered that since China cannot be excluded from Korea, then the Soviets will simply have to live with Pyongyang's efforts to play off Moscow and Beijing. (5) Should the Japanese presence be vigorously opposed? So far this has not been a major Soviet predicament, but as we have seen, there is potential for conflict. Soviet desires to 'neutralize' Japan do not always coincide with the DPRK's views on the use of the 'Tokyo card'.

It is therefore a basic conclusion that the Soviets have come to accept these predicaments of power as inevitable. Change cannot be ruled out, but it is hard to see where it will come. The Reagan administration is unlikely to take up the Carter policy of troop withdrawals from the ROK and there are no signs of the United States taking the ROK peace initiative of January 1982 more seriously than any of the previous ones. Neither is Japan able, or indeed likely, to strike out on its own with a path-breaking Korean initiative. There are however a few areas where some change is possible. First, a modicum of détente in Sino–Soviet relations[50] would lessen the intensity of the Soviet predicament. But it is already apparent that Moscow and Beijing do not fundamentally disagree on the need for peaceful unification of Korea. On the other hand, some have suggested that an improvement in general East–West relations is required before the Korean stalemate can be broken. The absence of any substantive improvement of local relations in the détente decade of the 1970s seems to argue against this view. In the final analysis, real change depends on the Korean actors themselves. The death of Kim Il-sung and a possible power struggle involving Chinese and Soviet support for different factions cannot be ruled out.[51] What is more challenging, and to return to the analogy of Palestine, the two Koreas have it within their power to break the deadlock and leave the great powers gasping. A Sadat-like 'pilgrimage' by Kim Il-sung to Seoul might just be the answer. At least it would provide some substance to Kim's otherwise vacuous personality cult.

Notes

[1]   US Department of State, Bureau of Intelligence and Research, *Korea–USSR Boundary*, International Boundary Study, no. 59 (15 December 1965).

[2]   Robert Simmons, *The Strained Alliance* (New York, Free Press, 1975), p. 3.

[3]   For cultural and historical details, see ibid., pp. 7–15; Gregory Henderson, *Korea: The Politics of the Vortex* (Cambridge, Harvard University Press, 1968); and Robert Scalapino and Chong-Sik Lee, *Communism in Korea* (Berkeley, Calif., University of California Press, 1972).

[4]   Harold Hinton, 'East Asia', in Kurt London (ed.), *The Soviet Union in World Politics* (Boulder, Colo., Westview Press, 1980); also R. Simmons, *Strained Alliance*; R. Scalapino and C.-S. Lee, *Communism in Korea*; and Wayne Kiyosaki, *North Korea's Foreign Relations* (New York, Praeger, 1976).

[5]   H. Hinton, 'East Asia'; Thomas Robinson, 'Soviet policy in east Asia', *Problems of Communism*, vol. 22, no. 6 (November–December 1973); Robert North, 'The Soviet far east: new centre of attention in the USSR', *Pacific Affairs*, vol. 51, no. 2 (Summer 1978); and John Despres, Lilita Dzirkals and Barton Whaley, *Timely Lessons of History: The Manchurian Model for Soviet Strategy* (Santa Monica, Calif., Rand Corporation, July 1976, R–1825–NA).

[6]   George Ginsburgs and Herta Ginsburgs, 'A statistical profile of the Korean community in the Soviet Union', *Asian Survey*, vol. 17, no. 10 (October 1977); V. Andreyev and V. Osipov, 'Relations of the USSR and the European socialist countries with the DPRK in the 1970's', *Far Eastern Affairs* (Moscow), no. 1 (1982); Radio Moscow in Korean, 8 July 1982, in BBC, *Summary of World Broadcasts* (*SWB*), *Soviet Union* (*SU*), 7078/A3/1–2; and *International Herald Tribune*, 10 June 1982.

[7]   Stephen Kaplan, *Diplomacy of Power* (Washington: Brookings Institution, 1981), p. 68; and Gabriel Kolko, *The Politics of War* (New York, Vintage, 1968), pp. 601–4.

[8]   Ibid., Chin Chung, *Pyongyang Between Peking and Moscow* (Montgomery, Ala., University of Alabama Press, 1978); and R. Simmons, *Strained Alliance*.

[9]   R. Simmons, *Strained Alliance*; William Stueck, 'The Soviet Union and the origins of the Korean War', *World Politics*, vol. 28, no. 4 (July 1976); Geoffrey Warner, 'The Korean War', *International Affairs*, vol. 56, no. 1 (January 1980); Mineo Nakajima, 'The Sino–Soviet confrontation: its roots in the international background of the Korean War', *Australian Journal of Chinese Affairs*, no. 1 (January 1979); Bruce Cummings, *The Origins of the Korean War* (Princeton, N.J., Princeton University Press, 1981); and Allen Whiting, *China Crosses the Yalu* (Stanford, Calif., Stanford University Press, 1960).

[10] Marshall Shulman, *Stalin's Foreign Policy Reappraised* (New York, Atheneum, 1969); also R. Simmons, *Strained Alliance*.

[11] For example, N. Ashurov and U. Alexeyev, 'Soviet–Korean cooperation', *Far Eastern Affairs* (Moscow), no. 1 (1980); and B. Mikhailov, '35 years of Soviet–Korean cooperation', ibid., no. 4 (1980).

[12] All details from William Zimmerman, 'The Korea and Vietnam Wars', in S. Kaplan, *Diplomacy of Power*; also S. Kaplan, *Diplomacy of Power*, pp. 90–2; R. Simmons, *Strained Alliance*, pp. 177–9; and W. Kiyosaki, *North Korea's Foreign Relations*, ch. 3.

[13] Kim Il-sung's requests for increased Soviet aid fell on unsympathetic ears as Stalin called Kim 'Mr' instead of 'Comrade' in confidential correspondence. See W. Zimmerman, 'Korea and Vietnam', and R. Simmons, *Strained Alliance*.

[14] Jane Shapiro, 'Soviet policy towards North Korea and Korean unification', *Pacific Affairs*, vol. 48, no. 3 (Fall 1975), pp. 348–51; Joungwon Kim, 'Pyongyang's search for legitimacy', *Problems of Communism*, vol. 20, nos. 1–2 (January–April 1971); T. Robinson, 'Soviet policy'; H. Hinton, 'East Asia'; and W. Kiyosaki, *North Korea's Foreign Relations*.

[15] All crises details from Abram Shulsky *et al.*, 'Coercive naval diplomacy, 1967–1974', in Bradford Dismukes and James McConnell (eds), *Soviet Naval Diplomacy* (New York, Pergamon, 1979), and Donald Zagoria and Janet Zagoria, 'Crises on the Korean peninsula', in S. Kaplan, *Diplomacy of Power*; also Byung Chul Koh, 'The *Pueblo* incident in perspective', *Asian Survey*, vol. 9, no. 4 (April 1969).

[16] Ibid., and Gerald Segal, *The Great Power Triangle* (London, Macmillan, 1982), ch. 4.

[17] See D. Zagoria and J. Zagoria, 'Korean peninsula', for arguments on why Kim's Vietnam link is the best explanation for grabbing the *Pueblo*.

[18] All details from ibid. and A. Shulsky *et al.*, 'Coercive naval diplomacy'.

[19] D. Zagoria and J. Zagoria, 'Korean peninsula'.

[20] Ibid.

[21] *Japan Times*, 24 January 1971, 9 July 1971, 19 June 1973, 25 June 1975, 2 November 1977, 26 April 1979, 14 July 1979; and *New York Times*, 22–25 April 1978.

[22]   D. Zagoria and J. Zagoria, 'Korean peninsula', pp. 400–401. Also William Watts *et al.*, *Japan, Korea and China* (Lexington, Mass. Heath, 1979), pp. 67–78; and H. Hinton, 'East Asia'.

[23]   N. Ashurov and U. Alexeyev, 'Soviet–Korean Cooperation'; B Mikhailov, '35 years'; and B. Moiseyev and N. Shubrikov, 'Sixth Congress of the Worker's Party of Korea: results and perspectives', *Far Eastern Affairs* (Moscow), no. 2 (1981); also W. Kiyosaki, *North Korea's Foreign Relations*; and Charles McLane, 'Korea in Russia's east Asian policy', in Young Kim (ed.), *Major Powers and Korea* (Silver Springs, Md., Research Institute on Korean Affairs, 1973).

[24]   R. Simmons, *Strained Alliance*; and C. Chung, *Pyongyang Between Peking and Moscow*.

[25]   On the war, see note 9.

[26]   R. Simmons, *Strained Alliance*, p. 32.

[27]   N. Ashurov and U. Alexeyev, 'Soviet–Korean cooperation'; and B. Mikhailov, '35 years'.

[28]   C. Chung, *Pyongyang Between Peking and Moscow*, pp. 15–17.

[29]   Ibid., chs 2 and 3; also J. Shapiro, 'Soviet policy'; C. McLane, 'Korea in Russia's east Asian policy'; Donald Zagoria, *The Sino–Soviet Conflict, 1956–61* (New York, Atheneum, 1973); and Robert Simmons, 'China's cautious relations with North Korea and Indochina', *Asian Survey*, vol. 11, no. 7 (July 1971).

[30]   R. Simmons, 'China's relations', pp. 631–3; also C. Chung, *Pyongyang Between Peking and Moscow*. Both China and the DPRK had bad experiences with the United Nations.

[31]   For example, B. Mikhailov, '35 years'; and Y. Ognev, 'The problem of strengthening peace in the Korean peninsula', *Far Eastern Affairs* (Moscow), no. 1 (1980).

[32]   Joseph Kun, 'North Korea: between Moscow and Peking', *China Quarterly*, no. 31 (July–September 1967); also J. Shapiro, 'Soviet policy'; and C. Chung, *Pyongyang Between Peking and Moscow*', ch. 6.

[33]   G. Segal, *Great Power Triangle*.

[34]   J. Kun, 'North Korea'; R. Simmons; 'China's relations'; and C. Chung, *Pyongyang Between Peking and Moscow*.

[35]   D. Zagoria and J. Zagoria, 'Korean peninsula', pp. 374, 382, 387, 388, 395; and A. Shulsky *et al.*, 'Coercive naval diplomacy'. The EC–121 may well have been monitoring the recent Sino–Soviet border clashes.

[36]   C. Chung, *Pyongyang Between Peking and Moscow*, chs 7 and 8; Chong-Sik Lee, 'The detente and Korea', in William Griffith (ed.), *The World and the Great-Power Triangles* (Cambridge, Mass., MIT Press, 1975); Ilpyong Kim, *Communist Politics in North Korea* (New York, Praeger, 1975), ch. 6; Donald Zagoria, 'Korea's future: Moscow's perspective', *Asian Survey*, vol. 17, no. 11 (November 1977); and *Daily Telegraph*, 12 February 1977. On trade, see also some data in B. Mikhailov, '35 years'.

[37]   Chong-Sik Lee, 'New paths for North Korea', *Problems of Communism*, vol. 26, no. 2 (March–April 1977); also *International Herald Tribune*, 24 January 1978. On China–ROK trade via Japan and Hong Kong, see BBC, *SWB*, *Far East (FE)*, 6621, 6623, 6672, and *Economist*, 28 February 1981.

[38]   Robert Scalapino, 'Current dynamics of the Korean peninsula', *Problems of Communism*, vol. 30, no. 6 (November–December 1981); and Ahn Byung-joon, 'South Korea and the communist countries', *Asian Survey*, vol. 20, no. 11 (November 1980); also *International Herald Tribune*, 12 March 1982.

[39]   For samples of Soviet attacks on China for collusion with the United States and the ROK, see N. Ashurov and U. Alexeyev, 'Soviet–Korean cooperation'; and Y. Ognev, 'The political crisis in South Korea and its origins', *Far Eastern Affairs* (Moscow), no. 2 (1981).

[40]   Y. Ognev, 'The problem of strengthening peace'. For a different view blaming China for discouraging unification by harping on 'the Soviet threat', see Ognev's article a year later, 'The political crisis in South Korea'.

[41]   M. Shulman, *Stalin's Foreign Policy Reappraised*, pp. 142–3; and R. Simmons, *Strained Alliance*.

[42]   H. Hinton, 'East Asia'; C. Chung, *Pyongyang Between Peking and Moscow*, ch. 6; and W. Kiyosaki, *North Korea's Foreign Relations*, pp. 9–10.

[43]   D. Zagoria and J. Zagoria, 'Korean peninsula', pp. 369, 380, 388.

[44]   C.-S. Lee, 'Detente and Korea'; and Seung Ko, 'North Korea's relations with Japan since detente', *Pacific Affairs*, vol. 50, no. 1 (Spring 1977); also Barnds, 'Two Koreas', pp. 28, 38.

[45]   Peggy Falkenheim, 'The impact of the Peace and Friendship Treaty on Soviet–Japanese relations', *Asian Survey*, vol. 19, no. 12 (December 1979).

[46]   Avigdor Haselkorn, 'Impact of Sino–Japanese treaty on the Soviet security strategy', *Asian Survey*, vol. 19, no. 6 (June 1979); also Donald Zagoria, 'Soviet policy and prospects in East Asia', *International Security*, vol. 5, no. 2 (Fall 1980).

[47]   See, for background, J. Shapiro, 'Soviet policy'; C. McLane, 'Korea in Russia's east Asian policy'; and *Japan Times*, 23 October 1973 and 2 September 1975. More recently, see H. Hinton, 'East Asia'.

[48]   B. Mikhailov, '35 years', p. 77; Y. Ognev, 'The problem of strengthening peace', pp. 21–2; Y. Ognev, 'The political crisis in South Korea', p. 108; and Y. Ognev, 'Glorious page in the history of the Korean people's liberation struggle', *Far Eastern Affairs* (Moscow), no. 2 (1979).

[49]   Adapted from Viktor Suvorov, *The Liberators: Inside the Soviet Army* (London, Hamish Hamilton, 1981), p. 154.

[50]   Gerald Segal, 'China's strategic debates', *Survival*, vol. 24, no. 2 (March–April 1982).

[51]   R. Scalapino, 'Current dynamics', pp. 24–5.

7 The Military Dimension of Soviet Policy
Lawrence Freedman

There can be little doubt that the USSR considers China a serious threa
to its security. This is not to say that Moscow feels nervous abou
Chinese aggression in the foreseeable future. On the contrary, it ha
every reason to feel reasonably secure. The point is only that in th
absence of a substantial military presence in its far eastern militar
districts the Soviet Union would feel vulnerable.

The Soviets have little difficulty in seeing China as a long-terr
menace. For a start the Chinese are, within Russian prejudices an
folklore, a menacing people. When the poet Yevtushenko wrote in th
1960s of 'the new Mongol warriors with bombs in their quivers' he wa
touching a responsive chord. The racial antipathy is accentuated by th
sheer size of the Chinese population, recent successes at controlling it
growth only serving as partial compensation for the fact that it i
adjacent and is already four times the size of the Soviet population
Russians take quantitative criteria very seriously.

For the Soviet leadership the ideological challenge posed by China i
also galling, though possibly not so much as before. There is no longer
Mao setting himself up as the legatee of the mantle of world leader i
Marxist ideology and contemptuously dismissing the bourgeois con
servatism of the modern Soviet state. Beijing has now had to drop th
charge of 'revisionism' against the USSR. Its own dramatic U-turn
have undermined confidence in its ideological judgement. In truth it n
longer seems interested in ideology for its own sake.

For a Soviet leadership that is still old enough to be smarting from
Tito's defection, memories of what it sees as Chinese ingratitude fo
Soviet help in the 1950s linger on and are mingled with resentment a
and the sustained and vitriolic tone of Chinese propaganda, barel
changing to reflect the shifts and turns of Beijing's foreign policy. Th
spectacle of Chinese leaders consorting with the 'imperialists', and eve
urging them to take a strong stand against the USSR is particularl
infuriating when it was the alleged feebleness of the Soviet response t

e 'US threat' that was a major cause of the initial Sino–Soviet split.

More serious is a traditional source of tension: an exceptionally long
d often ill-defined border, which is disputed by China against a
oviet claim that is quite strong in international law but involves an
nbarrassing support for Tsarist acquisitions. For a country with so
any disputed borders, this issue reverberates with awkward diplo-
atic implications. The Soviet stand has come to be one of uniform
transigence, to avoid dangerous precedents, and any exceptions are
rtainly not going to begin with China.

The disputed border would be no more than troublesome were it not
r the fact that it is so distant from the main centres of Soviet popula-
on but relatively close to key sources of raw materials. Both land and
ea communications across the country have been extremely difficult.
he key fact is that vital economic assets such as the Siberian oil and gas
elds are increasingly to be found east of the Urals. The usual statistic
quote is that whereas 80 per cent of Soviet energy is produced east of
e Urals, 80 per cent of the consumption is to the west.[1] Not only is the
opulation sparse but the loyalty of certain national groups to the centre
annot be taken for granted. The nature and extent of the Soviet
vestment in its eastern territories is described fully elsewhere in this
ook. Suffice it to say here that this investment is vital for the future
conomic health of the country and is therefore deserving of proper
rotection. It is not an enormous overstatement to say that in strategic
rms the Soviets may well view Siberia in the same way that the West
iews the Gulf.[2]

Furthermore, the USSR must also contend with the possibility of
olitical turbulence in China. The upheaval of the Cultural Revolution
larmed Moscow. Not only did it display a fanaticism and irrationality
nat Soviet leaders have long categorized as an infantile disorder rather
nan revolutionary enthusiasm but, in threatening the cohesion of the
eople's Republic, created a risk of private action by adventurist
roups, possibly in control of particular regions. The Cultural Revolu-
ion is now part of history, and there is no evident nostalgia in China for
he period, but the Soviet leaders are aware of China's economic and
ocial tensions (they harp on them enough in their propaganda) and
ust worry about failures in domestic policy creating renewed political
urmoil and even a revived interest in neighbourhood confrontation.
he new connection with the United States might have had some sort of
ivilizing' effect. Such an argument must always have been an awk-
vard one to push in Moscow. Latest Soviet pronouncements suggest
hat President Reagan is a bad influence on the Chinese, emphasizing a
oolish anti-Sovietism and discouraging recognition of shared interests
vith the USSR.[3]

The hopes invested in the immediate post-Mao leadership, indicated by an interlude in the polemics, were dashed when this leadershi stressed in Soviet eyes those aspects of Maoism that the Soviets foun most hateful: 'militant great-power-nationalism, unbridled heg monism in foreign policy, and anti-Sovietism and reliance on war an coercion as the key means of solving China's international and domest problems'.[4]

When Chinese forces are matched against Soviet forces it is hard believe that there is anything for the Kremlin to worry about. China forces are large but ill-equipped. With industrialization the quali should improve, but not at a pace that the USSR would be unable meet. However, the key factor in assessing the military balance is th local availability of men and equipment. The USSR's extended lines communication represent a logistical nightmare. The creation of a va military infrastructure in the Soviet far east in the early 1970s and th building of the new railway line have rendered the problem manage able. But Soviet leaders will be acutely aware that the maintenance their military position depends on a strong *local* garrison.

A Soviet threat to China?

The description of Soviet attitudes thus far has largely centred on possible Chinese threat to the USSR. What about a possible Sovi threat to China? The Chinese themselves do not claim to be particular threatened, insisting that the rich industrial countries to the USSR west provide it with far more tempting targets should it succumb expansionist urges. On the other hand they are anxious to see Sovi forces on the border step back and slim down and have described the as being excessively large for an ostensibly defensive force.

There seems no reason to suppose that the USSR nurtures seriou offensive objectives with regard to China. To the extent that it mai tains an offensive capability this is more likely for the purpose discouraging China from offensive action against those of its neigl bours to whom Moscow feels some sort of obligation. During th Indo–Pakistan war of 1971, it was made clear that dire consequence could follow any Chinese intervention on Pakistan's behalf. There wei similar rumblings during the Sino–Vietnam war of 1979, althoug Soviet protestations of support from Vietnam were largely declaratory To the extent that practical assistance was offered, the timing an nature of the relevant statements must have been amusingly remini cent to Beijing of the sort of qualified support it obtained during th 1958 offshore islands crisis.[5] Nevertheless, there is a capability punitive action that Beijing dare not ignore.

There seems no reason to believe that even the partial occupation China appears in Soviet dreams. Nor is it plausible that the USSI is contemplating some decisive showdown with China (as Edwar

Luttwak has recently suggested[6]). Apart from the fact that the current evidence suggests something quite the opposite, there is no reason to suppose that Moscow believes that the gains of some strike against China, which presumably would have to be nuclear, could compensate for the enormous political and military costs. There were certainly dark hints in the summer of 1969 when Moscow made an effort to convince Beijing that it was brewing something unpleasant. The rather public nature of the warnings as to imminent preemptive nuclear attacks may have been designed for purposes of intimidation, in which case they were successful, rather than as a prelude to an actual attack. That being said, many at the time, including members of the US government, took the warnings seriously.[7] The question is whether conditions are now better or worse than before. In the military sense it is by no means evident that they are worse, as will be discussed below, but the political calculations remain extremely negative for such an adventure. However much China exasperates the Soviet leadership, its likely response to the challenge is hope in some eventual political solution, perhaps with the ascendancy of a more 'realistic' and 'sober' faction in Beijing.

This does not mean a great interest in a return of China into the fold. Not only is it unrealistic to expect a revival of the 'Sino–Soviet bloc', but it is doubtful whether the USSR wants China back as an ally. To achieve this would probably involve promises of expensive economic assistance and even military assistance to a country with a capacity for trouble and an inability to defend itself properly without help. Moreover, the unpredictability of China has been sufficiently demonstrated to make the USSR wary of long-term commitments. It will take a dramatic change before the USSR dare remove its border defences to expose its eastern assets, given the likely delays it would face in reconstructing those defences should Sino–Soviet relations once again turn sour.

The overriding policy is one of military containment, including a capacity for occasional intimidation and, if necessary, limited punitive action. This is to be combined with a continual exploration of the possibilities for some sort of political understanding. So long as the first objective can be achieved then the second will be pursued by and large on Moscow's terms with few concessions to Chinese positions. The question which must concern us therefore is the ease with which the military objectives can be met. It will be argued that while the USSR should feel satisfied with its military position throughout the 1980s, resources constraints will encourage some thinning out of the far east garrison. This, plus continued tension with the West, still concentrating on Europe, encourages attempts to calm the Sino–Soviet dispute. However, it is doubtful that the USSR is willing to make sufficient concessions in its military or foreign policy to achieve this.

During 1982 there were definite signs that a serious effort was under way to sort out political differences. Wishing to devote all resources to an intensifying struggle with the United States, and with China suffering its own problems with the Reagan administration, the USSR took the initiative in seeking to improve relations with China. There had been virtually no dialogue between the two since the Soviet invasion of Afghanistan in December 1979, although increased trade and sporting contacts indicated an underlying interest in easing relations.

In March 1982 President Brezhnev pleaded for the end of hostilities. The following September, in a speech remarkably devoid of the customary recriminations, Brezhnev made the 'normalization' of relations with the People's Republic of China, on the basis of 'common sense, mutual respect and mutual advantage', the main priority of Soviet policy in Asia. A senior Soviet minister arrived in Beijing to begin exploratory talks. When the Chinese foreign minister arrived in Moscow in November for Brezhnev's funeral, the new Soviet leader, Mr Andropov, marked him out for special and visible attention, which appeared to be appreciated. Within Beijing there was evidence of some disagreement over how to handle this development. General Secretary Hu Yaobang was among the more positive, expressing a hope that 'obstacles' would be removed. The return to 'normal' Party-to-Party relations with the Moscow-oriented French Communist Party in October 1982 indicated a willingness to heal some of the divisions in the communist world. It has long been suggested that there might be some serious economic advantages in the two neighbours' working closer together.

However, the various viewpoints in Beijing will all expect movement on some basic security issues. The standard Chinese line has been that Moscow will be judged by actions more than words. The list of issues where actions are expected are formidable: the strength and proximity of Soviet forces along the border and in Mongolia; Soviet support for Vietnam; Soviet intervention in Afghanistan. The question we will address in this chapter is whether the Soviet interests which point to an accommodation with China are sufficient to override those interests and perceptions which will tend to qualify severely the concessions that Moscow will feel able to offer.

The Sino–Soviet military balance

Although the USSR began to build up its forces in the far eastern military regions after the 1963 polemics with China, these were essentially token forces. As the Cultural Revolution progressed, Soviet forces were further strengthened, but it was the arguments and clashes of 1968–9 that appeared to have convinced the Kremlin of the need for a well-developed capability.

There were a number of important and related features to the clashes of March 1969 over the Amur and Ussuri rivers. First, it was at about this time that the Chinese nuclear capability was becoming operational. The USSR certainly had a first-strike option – some 200 well-placed warheads would have rendered any retaliations virtually impossible. In 1968 about a quarter of Soviet medium- and intermediate-range missiles and aircraft were moved from bases facing Europe to bases facing China. The USSR also dropped a large number of hints that it was considering exercising the nuclear option. As we have already noted, the hints were sufficiently crude to suggest that the objective was mainly to remind the Chinese of the dangers of being over-provocative, and that in this the USSR may well have been successful. Chinese actions were certainly more circumspect during the later months of 1969 than in the early months, including the adoption of a less blasé attitude to becoming a nuclear power and a reorientation of the nuclear programme to make a regional capability the first priority.

However, while the Chinese were reminded of weaknesses in the nuclear sphere, the Soviets were reminded of their weaknesses in the conventional sphere. The lack of local reserves and stores and the highly vulnerable communications, including the Trans-Siberian Railway, appear to have dissuaded the Soviet general staff from 'taking on' the Chinese. Over the next four years the USSR took steps to correct these deficiencies. By 1970 the number of divisions facing the Chinese rose to about 30 (from only 18 in 1965) and it was soon approaching 40, with some 400,000 troops (China claimed 1 million but that assumed full-combat strength). The Soviets also constructed the infrastructure necessary for such a force – air bases, rail spurs, ammunition and fuel stores, barracks and so on. This large infrastructure has to be

Table 7.1 *Soviet ground-force divisions opposite China, 1965–82*

Military district	1965	1970	1975	1980	1982
Far eastern[a]	8	14	16	17	22
Transbaikal	5	8	9	9	9
Mongolia	—	2	2	4	4
Siberian	3	4	5	5	5
Central Asian	2	5	6	6	7
Total	18	33	38	41	47

[a] Excludes 1 division in Kamchatka and 2 on Sakhalin.
Source: *Strategic Survey, 1981–82* (London, IISS, 1982); *The Military Balance, 1982–83* (London, IISS, 1983).

remembered when considering proposals for moving Soviet force
back from the border area.

As can be seen from Table 7.1, in recent years there has been a
notable increase in the number of Soviet divisions facing China,
although the general level of readiness is lower than in the early 1970s.
The USSR has strengthened its forces in Mongolia, a matter of great
concern to the Chinese because of the threat thereby posed to their
industrial areas in the north, and in the far eastern district, which may
have something to do with Japan. In qualitative terms, the forces are
improving as a matter of course, benefiting from the advances that the
USSR is making in military technology. There is no reason to believe
that this trend will not continue into the 1980s.[8] Regarding maritime
forces, there is no contest in qualitative terms, despite the large size of
China's fleet.[9]

The current Sino–Soviet balance is therefore probably satisfactory
from Moscow's point of view. It must reckon that it can handle China
by itself in the coming years. The real worry has been over whether
China will be in alliance, tacit or direct, with some of the USSR's
adversaries. In 1978–9 there was obviously grave anxiety in Moscow
over the possibility of Western Europe, Japan and the United States
joining in some grand anti-Soviet conspiracy organized from Beijing.[10]
In quick succession China adopted ambitious modernization plans, and
generally took on a more dynamic appearance; concluded a peace treaty
with Japan; talked about arms deals with the Europeans; and 'norm-
alized' relations and started to talk military business with the United
States. It was common to talk of a Soviet fear of 'encirclement' so that
wherever it turned there would be a formidable enemy. However, the
problem was not the geographical spread of this coalition but its potential cumulative power, especially if within this coalition there was to be
transfer of power to China.

By now some of these fears must have eased. China has discovered
that the road to industrialization is long and difficult, and that the
imperatives of economic development often contradict those of military
development. The Western countries have all had their more exagger-
ated hopes of rich commercial pickings dashed. Chinese funds available
for high-technology imports do not stretch very far, and certainly not
far enough to include much military technology. With the West not in
the mood to make gifts of armaments and China, prudently, reluctant
to get too far into debt, arms deals have been few and far between. Even
the Reagan administration, favourably disposed towards any enemy of
the Soviet Union, has let Taiwan become a complicating factor in its
relations with China.

The inadequacy and backwardness of China's forces were illustrated
in early 1979 in the war with Vietnam. Reports in the West, which are

presumably an important source of intelligence on China for Moscow, describe equipment two or three generations behind that of the other major powers. Given this, and the low level of Western assistance, the USSR must reckon on the gap with China widening in its favour over the coming years.

Arms control: nuclear forces

There are some signs of a more realistic appreciation of the Chinese 'threat'. With a more modest threat perception, the USSR might well feel able to reduce its forces on its eastern border. A declining stock of men of military age and a generally stagnant economy are creating some sort of pressure for savings. Yet with relations with the West, and in particular the United States, as bad as ever, limited prospects for the sort of arms control that will significantly ease burdens, and substantial forces bogged down in Afghanistan, the far east offers one of the few likely areas where savings might be made.

If arms-control negotiations do make progress, then this may bring with it a requirement to cut nuclear forces. The United States has indicated its desire to include Soviet 'Intermediate' forces facing China and in the 'swing sites' just east of the Urals that can be targeted to both the East and the West in any ceiling agreed at the Intermediate Nuclear Force (INF) talks in Geneva. The USSR has so far resisted this, but if the prize was severe limits on NATO nuclear forces, it may feel that it could tolerate some limitations on its far eastern nuclear forces.[11]

The Chinese nuclear capabilities have not increased markedly, at least quantitatively. Moscow is now just about within reach. An ICBM has been tested, possibly as much for political as military reasons, but it is not yet operational. There has only recently been the first test of a submarine-launched ballistic missile,[12] normally considered to be the *sine qua non* of a second-strike capability, and an operational capability is distant. By contrast, Soviet nuclear capabilities have increased dramatically over the past decade, mainly through the fitting of multiple warheads to large launchers. Luttwak observes that 'a Soviet disarming counterforce offensive would have expended three-quarters of the Soviet ICBM arsenal in 1967 and as much as one-half of the more modern ICBMs as late as 1972, but would only require a small fraction (less than 10 per cent) of the Soviet ICBM arsenal now.'[13] One can read this, as does Luttwak, as evidence of the sort of strategic superiority that enables the Kremlin to contemplate decisive action. From another perspective it could serve as evidence that the sort of discounts that the USSR asks for in strategic arms negotiations with the United States because of the China factor could now be severely reduced, for there is much surplus capacity, so facilitating a new strategic arms agreement with the Americans.[14]

For its part, China has had a firm 'no first use of nuclear weapons' policy but otherwise has seen arms control as a device used by the superpowers in an attempt to maintain their nuclear monopoly. The partial test-ban treaty of 1963 and the 1970 non-proliferation treaty were both rejected on these grounds, and the general attitude towards SALT has been extremely dismissive. Thus, while some reduction of the nuclear threat to China is quite possible as an outcome of a US–Soviet agreement, this is not particularly high in the Chinese order of priorities simply because the amount of surplus capacity in the Soviet nuclear threat to China means that reductions would have only a marginal effect on the actual threat. Obviously removal of all SS–20s (which may have been designed originally with China in mind) as envisaged under President Reagan's 'zero option' would begin to make a significant difference, especially if combined with major reductions in intercontinental forces as envisaged under Reagan's START proposals. However, the Soviet response has hardly been encouraging, as it has sought to exclude non-European forces from an INF treaty and has proposed something less drastic for a strategic arms agreement. The conclusion must therefore remain that while a reduction in nuclear forces is as likely as any other sort of reduction, this will be accomplished as a result of US–Soviet rather than Sino–Soviet negotiations, and will probably not be to a level that will significantly alter Chinese security perceptions.

Arms control: conventional forces

For China the main concern is ground forces. Substantial reductions – of up to 75 per cent – have been spoken of as the prerequisite for any future rapprochement. Before examining the Soviet Union's ability to make concessions here it is worth noting the difficulties that might be faced, even with the best will in the world, in organizing conventional disarmament in the area. NATO and the Warsaw Pact, which can watch over each other's forces quite well, have faced tremendous problems in the Mutual Force Reductions talks in Vienna as a result of a serious discrepancy – some 150,000 troops – in their respective figures for Warsaw Pact strength. China's capacity to monitor Soviet force levels over the border is limited. Even with satellite photography this is an extremely imprecise art. And Chinese claims for the number of Soviet troops facing them have tended to be far higher than those suggested by official US sources or the International Institute for Strategic Studies (IISS). One reason for this may be a tendency to count divisions as if at full strength. According to the IISS, about half of the total force is only at Category 3 strength (i.e. about one-quarter full-combat strength) and only about a sixth are at Category 1 status (between three-quarters and full strength, complete with fighting vehicles).[15] There are thus limits to the extent to which serious force reductions could be accomplished simply by thinning out existing divisions. Not only would China be unconvinced that any real change had taken place, but there is not very much scope for much more thinning out.

The only sort of deal possible would involve movements of whole divisions out of the relevant military districts, but not to the extent that key areas are completely vacated. Intuitively a figure of some 30 divisions is a minimum and even that seems unlikely to be reached. It is also of note that reciprocal disarmament would be difficult to verify because of the comparative ease of Chinese lines of communication at the relevant points. Soviet forces are more confined, whereas Chinese could move in and out of an arms control guidelines area.

Not surprisingly, all of this has made it difficult for the USSR to promise major troop withdrawals. President Brezhnev has offered confidence-building measures of the sort discussed for Europe at the Madrid review conference of the Final Act of the Helsinki Conference on Security and Cooperation in Europe.[16] This would involve notification of large-scale manoeuvres, but would not require alteration to force levels.

It is important to recognize that the sort of concessions that the USSR might offer to achieve an agreement with China would be circumscribed by its military position. While possibly being willing to remove some divisions from the far east, the USSR would probably be unwilling to contemplate moving the actual bases. Having gone to the expense of their construction it will resist relocation, and given the critical importance of the infrastructure in the area it dare not tamper with it too extensively. Moving too far back might be seen to be conceding Chinese territorial claims, or even render it difficult to respond to mischief organized from the other side of the border. Furthermore, the USSR operates with offensive military doctrines, even when ostensibly on the defensive, and would not be willing to relinquish positions essential to this doctrine.[17] It is of note that Chinese doctrine, which involves drawing the enemy into territory so that it is forced to extend lines of communication, is much more compatible with a mutual pull-back of forces.

The USSR would not wish to lose its capacity for intimidation, at least so long as the political differences between the USSR and China remain.[18] It is doubtful whether the Soviet general staff, given its trouble in Afghanistan, can bear even to think about the problems of invading and occupying all of China. Nevertheless, there have been and could be occasions when some punitive action, or the threat of such, would seem necessary to Moscow.

At the moment, it would not be very difficult to 'teach Beijing a lesson' should the need arise. Significant Chinese assets are in reach so that long-term economic damage could be inflicted before a speedy withdrawal. Hesitations would not result from doubts about the Soviet ability to prevail eventually in such a conflict. They would most likely result from the fact that large numbers can still cause qualitatively superior force problems. There are analogies with some of the USSR's own battles against the Germans. In the Sino–Vietnam conflict, the Chinese did at times indulge (with varying success) in 'human wave' tactics to overwhelm better-equipped Vietnamese forces. All the more reason, in such circumstances, to ensure quick action before the cumbersome Chinese military machine could swing into action. The USSR must also consider the possibility of China acting in an opportunist manner to exploit a US–Soviet confrontation. It is of note that in 1979 a theatre-level command was established in the Soviet far east to allow for significant operational autonomy in the event of a two-front war.[19]

Given all this, it is going to be generally difficult to get agreement to remove forces from front-line positions, and particularly so with the four divisions in Mongolia, which have been singled out by China for special mention and occupy a crucial role in menacing the most valuable segments of Chinese territory. The conclusion must be that the Soviet flexibility, when it comes to the actual disposition of its forces, is not that great for both infrastructural and doctrinal reasons.

Furthermore, its force structure in the east is not organized wholly with China in mind. Take, for example, its Pacific fleet of some 120 submarines (25 nuclear) and 85 major surface combatants. This opens up options for amphibious landings or disruption of all activity along China's coastal waters. Yet the structure of the Pacific fleet is designed with the United States in mind more than China. The current US stress on sea power will not permit any change in this area. Indeed, although the United States may have more direct interest in the Indian Ocean, all of its Pacific allies are dependent on sea lines of communication.

In general the United States still maintains a substantial presence in the area – in South Korea, Japan, the Philippines and Guam. The USSR also has to take increasing account of Japan. Japan is taking a growing interest in military matters and is improving its self-defence forces. It is unlikely to be able to do much in the maritime sphere though that is likely to be the most important in strategic terms. However, Soviet planners must be aware of the enormous potential for a military build-up made possible by Japan's economic and technological strength. At the moment, the Soviet Union tends to stress the possibility of good relations with Japan, which are undermined by the need also to stress the problems, including the risk of retaliation, posed by the Japanese hosting so many US bases. The possibility for improved relations has been impaired by its reluctance to give way at all on the northern islands, claimed by Japan and which the USSR holds and has fortified. The refusal to budge from these islands serves as a striking example of the priority attached by the USSR to the territorial status quo and strategic requirements.[20]

Conclusions

The conclusion must be that the USSR will find it difficult to make substantial reductions in military capabilities by way of concessions to China in an effort to improve relations. It may be possible to reduce the number of divisions, by around a third. It is even possible that some reductions might result from force-planning decisions made in Moscow as a result of personnel and other resource shortages. Nuclear forces might be cut as a result of a US–Soviet agreement. But the basic location and organization of Soviet far eastern forces are unlikely to be changed and it may even be difficult to demonstrate convincingly that real cuts have been made.

What then of the other two areas where China has demanded action? There is some debate about how much China actually cares about Afghanistan as its own border with Afghanistan is rather small. However, to Beijing, the move into Afghanistan helped strengthen Moscow's position as a regional power and, combined with the support of Vietnam, increased the danger of China's encirclement.[21] There are indications that the USSR would like to get out of Afghanistan but the political problems of an honourable withdrawal are great, particularly when it comes to agreeing on the sort of regime to be permitted in Kabul. The current Soviet effort of some 100,000 seems sufficient to contain the rebels but not to defeat them. It is a level that can be sustained for some time and probably Moscow has accepted that it now has a long-term commitment on its hands.

The Vietnam question is more complex. When the USSR began to put out feelers to China the Vietnamese became alarmed that they were going to be ditched and President Truong Chinh hurried to Moscow. There he secured agreement that third-party interests would not be adversely affected by any Sino–Soviet rapprochement in return for which he offered a willingness to contemplate 'Sino–Vietnamese' rapprochement. The Chinese response was to make renewed allegations of border violations.[22] Again it is in Soviet interests to achieve a settlement – the cost of supporting Vietnam's shaky economy, made shakier by its military involvement in Kampuchea and Laos, must be approaching US $2 billion. Such support also encourages the hostility of the ASEAN countries.[23] But the diplomatic problems of achieving what will seem to Moscow to be an honourable settlement are forbidding. As things stand Indochina provides the most likely trigger to a general worsening of Sino–Soviet relations. The risk of a Vietnamese incursion into Thailand, chasing Kampuchean guerrillas, has subsided but still remains. The Sino–Vietnamese border is still tense and the subject of regular allegations from both sides. The USSR's 1978 treaty with Vietnam ties the two states close to one another, and with Vietnamese suspicions of the USSR's trustworthiness heightened by the latter's limited support during the 1979 Sino–Vietnamese War, Moscow will find it difficult to impose a settlement on Hanoi without resorting to heavy-handed economic pressure. The choice between Hanoi and Beijing would be difficult even if Beijing was being conciliatory at every other point of contention. In the absence of any concessions from Beijing, Moscow may well feel that it has no choice and that it must continue to build upon the heavy investment in Vietnam.

None of this is very encouraging for a fundamental Sino–Soviet rapprochement. The concessions that both would have to make, in a highly visible manner, make a new treaty of friendship and cooperation unlikely. What is more likely is a tacit understanding to tone down the polemics, build up trade and other contacts, and generally reduce the temperature. As a final point it could be argued from the West's point of view that this is preferable to full rapprochement as it will ensure that a large number of Soviet forces will still be tied down in the east. However, if China was able to achieve dramatic and positive changes in its position with regard to Afghanistan and Vietnam as the price of rapprochement, then the West could also be a beneficiary, as two of the barriers to an improvement in East–West relations would also have been removed.

Notes

[1]   Alan Smith, 'Soviet dependence on Siberian resource development', in *Soviet Economy in a New Perspective*, a compendium of papers presented to the Joint Economic Committee of Congress (Washington, DC: USGPO, 14 October 1976).

[2]   For a similar view, see 'Siberia and the Soviet presence in east Asia', *Strategic Survey 1981–82* (London, IISS, 1982): 'During the remainder of this century, Siberia will become an increasingly important asset in Soviet national perspectives and security concerns' (p. 107).

[3]   *Pravda*, in July 1982, described a US intention to 'bleed white' both the USSR and China to weaken them both; see *International Herald Tribune*, 8 October 1982.

[4]   Seweryn Bailer, 'The Soviet perspective', in Herbert J. Ellison (ed.), *The Sino–Soviet Conflict: A Global Perspective* (Seattle, Washington, University of Washington Press, 1982), p. 35.

[5]   See Daniel Tretiak, 'China's Vietnam War and its consequences', *China Quarterly*, December 1979. Tretiak suggests that if China had pushed at the limits too hard the USSR would probably have felt obliged to intervene.

[6] Edward N. Luttwak, 'The PRC in Soviet grand strategy', in Douglas T. Stuart and William T. Tow (eds), *China, The Soviet Union and the West: Strategic and Political Dimensions in the 1980s* (Boulder, Colo., Westview Press, 1982): 'the Soviet leadership may . . . make the forceful solution of its "China problem" the overriding priority of its years of strategic opportunity of the 1980s' (p. 273).

[7] Henry Kissinger, *The White House Years* (London, Weidenfeld & Nicolson, 1979), pp. 183–4.

[8] For a projection of likely improvements to Soviet forces in east Asia, see the appendix to Paul Dibb, 'Soviet capabilities, interests and strategies in east Asia in the 1980s', *Survival*, vol. 24, no. 4 (July–August 1982), pp. 160–1.

[9] See Donald Daniel, 'Sino–Soviet relations in naval perspective', in D.T. Stuart and W.T. Tow (eds), *China, the Soviet Union and the West*.

[10] Gerald Segal, 'The Soviet Union and the great power triangle', in Gerald Segal (ed.), *The China Factor* (London, Croom Helm, 1982).

[11] See Lawrence Freedman, 'The dilemma of theatre nuclear arms control', *Survival*, vol. 23, no. 1 (January–February 1981).

[12] *International Herald Tribune*, 18 October 1982.

[13] E.N. Luttwak, 'The PRC in Soviet grand strategy', p. 268, note 6.

[14] Ray Garthoff suggests that the USSR had a figure of 300 missiles in mind for China during the SALT I negotiations; see Raymond L. Garthoff, 'SALT and the Soviet military', *Problems of Communism*, vol. 24 (January–February 1975).

[15] *Strategic Survey 1981–82*, p. 105.

[16] L.I. Brezhnev, *Report of the Central Committee of the CPSU to the XXVI Congress of the Communist Party of the Soviet Union* (23 February 1981).

[17] It is of note that Soviet analyses of the 1945 'Manchuria' campaign, considered as a model of 'lightning war', increased markedly as the Sino–Soviet conflict hotted up. See Lilita I. Dzirkals, *'Lightning War' in Manchuria: Soviet Military Analysis of the 1945 Far Eastern Campaign* (Santa Monica, Calif., Rand Corporation, January 1976), p. 89.

[18] See Kenneth Hunt, 'Sino–Soviet theater comparisons', and William C. Green and David S. Yost, 'Soviet military options regarding China', both in B.T. Stuart and W.T. Tow, *China, the Soviet Union and the West*.

[19] Paul Dibb, 'Soviet capabilities, interests and strategies in east Asia', p. 155.

[20] Donald Hellmann, 'The impact of the Sino–Soviet dispute on northeast Asia', in H.J. Ellison (ed.), *The Sino–Soviet Conflict*.

[21] Yaacov Vertzberger, 'Afghanistan in China's policy', *Problems of Communism*, vol. 31, no. 3 (May–June 1982).

[22] *International Herald Tribune*, 14 October 1982.

[23] Michael Leifer, *Conflict and Regional Order in South–East Asia*, Adelphi Paper 162 (London, IISS, 1980).

8 The Economic Dimension of Soviet Policy
*Kazuyuki Kinbara**

The aim of this chapter is to spell out some of the features of Soviet economic relations with Far Eastern states, with particular reference to Japanese–Soviet economic relations, and to discuss their prospects over the next decade. I shall also try to consider the political implications of Soviet economic relations with these countries, for although this chapter deals with the economic dimension of Soviet–Far Eastern relations, Soviet foreign trade, which is always conducted in the form of a state monopoly, can only adequately be discussed in the context of overall Soviet foreign policy. It is also useful to raise the question of whether or not the USSR is likely to attempt to exert influence over Far Eastern states by using economic ties as a political tool.

It would be misleading, however, to perceive the application of any comprehensive Soviet foreign economic policies to all countries in the Far East. Above all, it should be stressed that Japan's position is unique in many respects. There is no doubt that trade links with that country are exceptionally important for the Soviet economy. This fact is closely related to the large gap between the Japanese economy and the other national economies in the Far East in terms of both size and stage of economic development. Taking the figures for 1981, Japan's share in Soviet foreign trade in the Far East was 63.5 per cent, while the corresponding share of China was 3.7 per cent, Mongolia 21.7 per cent and the Democratic People's Republic of Korea (DPRK) 11.1 per cent. A simple comparison of total volumes of trade may not, however, suffice to explain the significance for the USSR of trade relations with Japan. Viewed in the context of East–West trade, Japan is one of the chief suppliers among industrialized capitalist states of Western technology to the USSR. Furthermore, Japan is the only country in the Far East that can offer the prospect of export markets large enough to

*The author is greatly indebted to Mr Keisuke Suzuki, Mr Michael Kaser and Dr Gerald Segal for the advice and stimulation they have given him.

absorb a substantial portion of Siberian natural resources. The key element of economic relations between the two countries is business based upon reciprocal interests. Incidentally, barter trade, which is common to Soviet trade with the other Far Eastern states, takes just a few per cent of the total turnover of Japanese–Soviet trade.

On the other hand, Mongolia and the DPRK, which receive various forms of economic aid from the USSR, should primarily be regarded as economic beneficiaries, although the degree to which each is dependent upon the Soviet Union is very different. Sino–Soviet trade relations have been at a relatively low ebb since the political rift between the two countries in the late 1950s which brought to an end the massive Soviet economic assistance to China.

On the political front, the positions of local states vis-à-vis the USSR also vary. Japan, whose political relationship with the USSR is cool, seems to keep the Soviet Union cautiously at arm's length. China and Mongolia are at opposite extremes in their relations with the USSR, while the DPRK is somewhere between the two poles.

In this chapter, Soviet trading partners in the Far East are taken to be Japan, China, Mongolia and the DPRK. Direct economic relations between the Republic of Korea (ROK) and the USSR, the level of which is very near to zero, are not dealt with here.[1]

Japanese–Soviet economic relations

Historical review of post-war Japanese–Soviet trade

It is nearly a quarter of a century since the signing of the Japanese–Soviet treaty of commerce and the Japanese–Soviet trade payment agreement in December 1957 which led to a rapid increase in the volume of trade between the two countries throughout the late 1950s and the early 1960s (see Table 8.1). Post-war Japanese–Soviet trade may be divided according to the nature of the trade into three time periods: (1) trade supervised by the general Allied headquarters between 1946 and 1949, (2) private, non-agreement trade between 1950 and 1957, and (3) government-agreement trade from 1958.[2]

During the early post-war period (1946–9), when trade was supervised by the General Headquarters of the Allied Occupation Forces, Japan exported wooden boats, steam engines, freight cars, fishing nets, rope and other materials to the USSR. Imports to Japan from the USSR were mainly Sakhalin coal. Such trade was temporarily conducted on an open account basis in coordination with the Soviet representatives at the General Headquarters but ceased when the open accounts were transferred to the Bank of Japan at the end of 1949.

The years between 1950 and 1957 were the most difficult ones for Japanese–Soviet trade, reflecting the Cold War, when there were

Table 8.1 *Japanese–Soviet trade, 1946–81* (1000s of US dollars[a])

Nature of trade	Year	Japanese exports	Imports to Japan	Total volume
General-headquarters-supervised trade	1946	24	0	24
	1947	140	2,004	2,144
	1948	4,385	2,670	7,055
	1949	7,360	1,933	9,293
Private non-agreement trade	1950	723	738	1,461
	1951	0	28	28
	1952	150	459	609
	1953	7	2,101	2,108
	1954	39	2,249	2,288
	1955	2,710	3,070	5,780
	1956	760	2,860	3,620
	(19 October, restoration of Japanese–Soviet relations)			
	1957	9,294 (100)	12,324 (100)	21,618 (100
	(6 December, treaty of commerce and trade payment agreement)			
Government-agreement trade	1958	18,100 (195)	22,150 (180)	40,250 (186
	1959	23,026 (248)	39,490 (320)	62,516 (298
	(1960–2 trade payment agreement)			
	1960	59,976 (645)	87,025 (706)	147,001 (680
	1961	65,380 (703)	145,409 (1,180)	210,789 (975
	1962	149,390 (1,607)	147,309 (1,195)	296,699 (1,3?
	(1963–5 trade payment agreement)			
	1963	158,136 (1,701)	161,940 (1,314)	320,076 (1,48
	1964	181,810 (1,956)	226,729 (1,840)	408,539 (1,89
	1965	168,358 (1,811)	240,198 (1,949)	408,556 (1,89
	(1966–70 trade payment agreement)			
	1966	214,022 (2,308)	300,361 (2,437)	514,383 (2,37
	1967	157,688 (1,697)	453,918 (3,683)	611,606 (2,82
	1968	179,018 (1,926)	463,512 (3,761)	642,530 (2,97
	1969	268,247 (2,886)	461,563 (3,745)	729,810 (3,37
	1970	340,932 (3,668)	481,038 (3,903)	821,970 (3,80
	(1971–5 trade payment agreement)			
	1971	377,267 (4,059)	495,880 (4,024)	873,147 (4,03
	1972	504,179 (5,425)	593,906 (4,819)	1,098,085 (5,07
	1973	484,210 (5,210)	1,077,701 (8,745)	1,561,911 (7,22
	1974	1,095,642 (11,789)	1,418,143 (11,507)	2,513,785 (11,6
	1975	1,626,200 (17,497)	1,169,618 (9,491)	2,795,818 (12,9
	(1976–80 trade payment agreement)			
	1976	2,251,894 (24,230)	1,167,441 (9,473)	3,419,335 (15,8
	1977	1,933,877 (20,808)	1,421,875 (11,537)	3,355,752 (15,5
	1978	2,502,195 (26,923)	1,441,723 (11,698)	3,943,918 (18,2
	1979	2,461,464 (26,484)	1,910,681 (15,504)	4,372,145 (20,2
	1980	2,778,233 (29,893)	1,859,866 (15,091)	4,638,099 (21,4
	(1981–5 trade payment agreement)			
	1981	3,259,415 (35,070)	2,020,706 (16,379)	5,280,121 (24,4

[a] Figures in parentheses are indices of trade change (1957 = 100).

Source: Soren Too Boeki Kai, 'Nisso Boeki Tokei', *Soren Too Boeki Chosa Geppo* (1981).

either commercial treaties nor trade and payment agreements between the two countries. In particular, the first three years of the 1950s were the most stagnant period in the history of post-war Japanese–Soviet trade, with no Japanese exports and only a small amount of coal imported from Sakhalin in 1951. In the middle of 1948 the US government started to enlist the cooperation of the West European governments in its embargo against the communist states on strategic goods. This culminated in the establishment in November 1949 of Cocom (the Coordinating Committee) which Japan joined in 1952.[3] In July 1951, just one year after the outbreak of the Korean War, the United States notified the USSR of its denunciation of the US–Soviet treaty of Commerce, concluded in 1937.

After the armistice that ended the Korean War in July 1953, the USSR called for an expansion of trade with the Japanese business community, and in June 1954 Soviet trade organizations and Japanese companies reached a provisional agreement for a trade exchange of US 80 million over the remainder of 1954 and 1955.[4] The Japanese exports indicated in the agreement were dominated by boats and ships, which was welcomed by the Japanese shipbuilding industry, suffering from a recession at that time. As for imports from the USSR, wood was the main item in the provisional agreement. However, only US $7.4 million, less than one-tenth of the amount of trade indicated in the agreement, materialized. The cancellation of the Soviet purchase of Japanese ships was considered one of the major reasons for the poor results of the agreement. In sum, it may be said that the development of Japanese–Soviet trade in the first decade of the post-war period was in general insignificant in terms of both value and volume.

In October 1956 Japan and the USSR restored diplomatic relations in the form of the Japanese–Soviet joint declaration. Prior to the declaration, in August 1956, Soviet Foreign Minister Shepilov proposed to the Japanese ambassador in Moscow that restoration of diplomatic relations would make it possible to increase Japanese–Soviet trade up to 1 billion roubles in total within the next five years. Subsequently the USSR launched a campaign to promote Japanese–Soviet trade through *Pravda* and radio broadcasts.

In accordance with the declaration, the Japanese–Soviet treaty of commerce and the Japanese–Soviet trade payment agreement were signed between the governments in December 1957 after three months of negotiations. Although the original intention of the Japanese government was only to negotiate the trade payment agreement, the treaty of commerce was also concluded at the wish of the USSR. The level of trade in 1957, six times that in 1956, clearly indicated the effect of these documents. The Japanese–Soviet trade payment agreement has been renewed at differing intervals (see Table 8.1). Against this background,

the trade between the two countries showed a favourable developmen
throughout the 1960s with many large-scale trade fairs held in Moscov
and several high-level economic missions.

The most important events in Japanese–Soviet economic relations i
the 1960s were the establishment of bilateral economic committees i
the two countries and the subsequent emergence of long-term an
national-level collaborative projects in Siberia (named Japan–Sovie
Siberian development projects), which will be discussed below. In Jul
1965 Japanese business leaders, including the chairman of the Japanes
Chamber of Commerce and the chairman of Keidanren (the Federatio
of Economic Organizations), and the Soviet Ministry of Foreign Trad
agreed to set up bilateral economic committees as a step towards furthe
promotion of economic relations. These were named the Japan–Sovie
Business Cooperation Committee, on the Japanese side, and th
Soviet–Japan Business Cooperation Committee, on the Soviet side.

The Soviet Professor D. V. Petrov explained the background of th
establishment of the committees as follows:

As both countries deepened their understanding of the other's economic situa
tion, they came to share the common view that they should seek new ways fo
the further development of economic exchange between them. This tendenc
led to the establishment of organizations which would handle fundamenta
issues concerning the economic relations between them.[5]

This interpretation more or less represented the view of the Japanes
business leaders concerned as well as the Soviet Ministry of Foreigr
Trade.

According to the carefully worded rules of the Japan–Soviet Busines:
Cooperation Committee, its purpose is to deepen mutual understand
ing and friendship between the Japanese business community and it
counterpart on the Soviet side and to promote economic relation:
including trade and technological cooperation between the two coun
tries. Apart from this rather abstract purpose, the actual function of th
Committee since its establishment has been mainly promoting anc
organizing Japan–Soviet Siberian development projects. In fact, the
emergence of the Committee was an important impetus to introducing a
new aspect to the economic relations between the two states in the form
of collaborative projects in Siberia.

The level of Japanese–Soviet trade in the first half of the 1970:
continued to increase even more rapidly than in the 1960s. In particula
Japanese exports of machinery and equipment related to Siberiar
collaborative projects, steel and large-scale plants contributed greatly
to the rapid growth of trade. As a result, the trade balance between the
two countries was reversed in 1975, after an excess of Japanese imports

for many years. Japan has enjoyed a favourable balance of trade with the USSR ever since.

The euphoria of expanding trade culminated in a summit meeting between Soviet President Brezhnev and Japanese Prime Minister Tanaka in Moscow in October 1973. Although the meeting was not primarily an economic summit, it had two significant implications in the history of Japanese–Soviet economic relations since the conclusion of the treaty of commerce in 1957. First, it is said that they agreed at the meeting that the channel on the Japanese side for negotiations on Japanese–Soviet Siberian development projects should be exclusively the Japan–Soviet Business Cooperation Committee. Thus the private committee was formally authorized by the heads of the two governments. Second, Tanaka promised that the Japanese government would financially support Siberian collaborative projects once both committees had agreed to cooperate on them. Given that the Japanese government is usually reluctant to commit itself to anything with regard to trade relations with the USSR, this remark by Tanaka was exceptionally positive and clear. Moreover, during the year following the summit meeting, this proved not to be mere lip-service. In April 1974 the protocol for a bank loan of US $1.1 billion by the Japanese Export and Import Bank (the EXIM Bank) to the USSR to finance three Siberian projects was signed between the two governments. It may be said that this protocol opened up a new dimension in the financial aspect of Japanese–Soviet trade relations. Afterwards, bank loans, meaning direct credits from the Japanese government to the USSR, began to be adopted not only for Siberian projects but also for many large-scale Soviet import deals with Japan, playing a large role in facilitating Japanese steel and plant exports to the country.[6]

However, in 1977 the level of trade slightly decreased compared with the previous year, for the first time in 20 years. The subsequent pace of trade growth has been relatively slow.

Japan–Soviet Siberian development projects

Since the emergence of Japan–Soviet Siberian development projects in the late 1960s, project trade has become an important element in the trade between the two states. The usual pattern of project trade is as follows. When both committees agree on cooperation over a Siberian project, usually after years of negotiations, a general agreement is concluded between them which stipulates the framework of the project. The Japanese side, on the basis of the agreement, extends credit with which the USSR purchases machinery and equipment needed for the project and embarks upon the specific development of natural resources with which the project is concerned. The amount of credit advanced by Japan is believed to be in most cases about one-third of the total development cost of the project. After a period of operation, normally lasting several years, the Soviet side in return starts supplying a portion of the developed natural resources to Japan and pays back credit at the same time. This pattern, which is termed a 'compensation deal' by both the parties concerned, is common to almost all the Siberian collaborative projects between the two countries.

It is understood that the biannual joint conference between the two committees has been not only the most important occasion for official negotiation on projects but also the barometer of the overall state of Japanese–Soviet economic relations. The first session of the joint conference was held in Tokyo in March 1966 and the last one, the eighth session, was in Moscow in September 1979.[7]

Since the committees were set up in the second half of the 1960s, three projects have emerged: the First-Stage Soviet Far East Forest Resources Development Project, the Vrangel Port Construction Project and the Chip and Pulp Development Project. These three projects can be called 'earlier-stage projects', and they have common features which may serve to clarify the difference between them and the projects that emerged in the 1970s. First, the scale of the first three projects was much smaller than that of projects in the 1970s. For example, even the Forest Resources Development Project, which was the largest of the three, was less than half the size of the smallest project in the 1970s. Second, the form of credit adopted for the three earlier projects was supplier's credit. By contrast, almost all credit adopted for the projects in the 1970s were bank loans. Third, none of these three projects was related to energy resources such as oil, natural gas or coal. On the other hand, the projects which appeared in the early 1970s were all concerned with developing energy resources.

The first half of the 1970s may be characterized as a period of intensive development of Siberian collaborative projects. In fact, all but one of the general agreements for Siberian collaborative projects in operation today were concluded in this period. These continuing projects are for the development of coal in southern Yakutia, the development of natural gas in Yakutia and prospecting for oil and gas on the continental shelf off Sakhalin; only the Second-Stage Soviet Far East Forest Resources Development Project has been completed – at the end of 1979 – and the third stage was started in 1981.[8]

When particular attention is paid to the overall process of Japan–Soviet Siberian development projects, the first half of the 1970s presents a contrast to the second half of that decade, which saw no new projects.[9] This was due mainly to domestic economic problems in the USSR, rather than to the deterioration of political relations between the two states. In this respect, it may be worth noting that the USSR has always been more positive and active than Japan in strengthening onomic links between them in the post-war period, and that in most ses it was the Soviets who took the initiative in doing so. The Japanese ere sometimes cautious, mainly as a result of political considerations. s mentioned above, even in the Cold War period, and before the storation of diplomatic relations, the USSR was keen on an expansion trade with Japan. It is therefore likely that the USSR failed to opose a new project in the latter half of the 1970s, not because it did ot wish to do so, but because it could not afford to for lack of capital d a workforce for such projects.

roblems and prospects

he political and economic factors expected to have considerable influ- ce over the future trend of Japanese–Soviet economic relations are of urse interrelated. Nevertheless, I shall discuss political factors and onomic factors separately in order to clarify the set of problems ising from each.

One of the major political factors may be the probability of the USSR sing economic leverage for political purposes. Some fear that the SSR will stop supplying energy resources to Japan in an attempt to ert political pressure. Professor J. Nye of Harvard University main- ined that depending on the USSR for energy resources could become new threat to Japan.[10] Taking into account that the supply of energy sources (liquefied natural gas (LNG), coking coal) from Siberia as a sult of current collaborative projects will start in the latter half of the 980s, this warning may be worth listening to.

However, there seem to be several reasons for supporting the conjec- re that the USSR is quite unlikely to use economic leverage over apan as a political weapon in the foreseeable future. In the first place, e amount of energy that Japan imports from the USSR is very small – ss than 1 per cent of its total domestic demand. It is computed that here the supply of energy resources from Siberia is established, the ossible maximum rate of dependency upon the USSR for LNG will be st 6 or 7 per cent and for coking coal, 9 per cent.[11] As for oil imported om the USSR, the amount has been and will be negligible. Therefore, sudden all-out cut-off of supply from the USSR would not cause a rious problem for Japan. As for wood imports, which take the largest hare in total Japanese imports from the USSR (see Table 8.2) and hich also account for about 15 per cent of its total domestic demand r wood, Japan could manage to find alternative supply sources with- ut much difficulty, most probably in North America, in the event of a oviet embargo. After all, wood is not as vital to the national economy s energy resources. As Allen S. Whiting aptly put it,[12] the Soviet upply of natural resources is useful, and perhaps very useful under ertain circumstances, but not essential to the Japanese economy.

Table 8.2   *Shift in percentage shares of principal items in Japanese–Soviet trade 1960–80*

	1960–5	1966–70	1971–5	1976–80
A Japanese Exports				
Textile goods	15.0	29.5	14.6	7.3
Chemicals	5.7	12.3	10.6	8.6
Steel manufactures	20.3	13.8	32.4	36.3
Machinery	49.0	32.6	32.2	36.6
(Ordinary machinery)	21.6	19.5	19.8	24.1
(Electrical machinery)	2.6	4.6	4.3	5.4
(Transport machinery)	23.6	6.7	7.0	6.2
B Japanese Imports				
Food	2.7	1.8	2.5	4.2
Raw materials	29.2	51.8	57.2	52.0
Wood	21.8	33.7	37.6	37.4
Mineral fuel	36.7	19.1	14.9	16.6
Coal	8.6	8.6	9.0	9.2
Crude oil and oil products	28.0	10.5	5.9	7.4
Chemicals	5.4	2.5	3.0	2.4
Machinery	0.9	0.8	0.8	1.9
Pig iron	16.6	8.6	0.7	—
Non-ferrous metals	7.9	14.6	17.7	16.2

Source: Japan–Soviet Business Cooperation Committee (Federation of Economic Organizations).

Taking these facts into account, embargoes against the sales of natural resources to Japan of any kind may not be an effective weapon for the USSR. On the other hand, the costs of such a measure for the USSR would be enormous. Not only could the USSR not anticipate further Japanese cooperation in Siberian development but also Soviet credit and its reputation for reliability as a trade partner would be lost in Western business communities. Furthermore, the USSR would lose the largest export market in the Far East for its natural resources, and earning hard currency as much as possible through exporting natural resources to Japan is particularly needed since long-term and low interest credit from the West has become scarcer. It is patently obvious that the USSR would be unable to find an alternative export market in the Far East as large as Japan. It should be emphasized here that hard currency is increasingly vital in keeping the battered Soviet economy going, in terms of both purchasing Western technology and importing grains.

As for the feasibility of the Soviets using the stoppage of imports of Japanese goods as a political tool, such a measure would be even more counter-productive for the USSR. What the USSR is importing from Japan, mainly machinery and steel (see Table 8.2), is essential to the Soviet economy, particularly for Siberian development, the economic significance of which is rapidly growing. When Japanese–Soviet trade is viewed as a whole, in the context of the aggregate of Japan's foreign trade, the level of Japan's trade with the USSR is constantly low. It has been less than 3 per cent per annum over the past two decades. Figures for 1981 show that the USSR counted for just 2.1 per cent of Japan's total exports that year, and 1.4 per cent of its imports. In short any attempt to achieve political goals by manipulating trade relations with Japan would be not only ineffective, but also severely damaging to the USSR.

Finally it should be added that the USSR is a reliable trading partner in the sense that it has historically rarely stopped supplying natural resources to the West for a political reason. It was quick to condemn the grain embargo by President Carter in 1980, and from time to time decries the policy of using trade for political purposes.[13] In effect, the USSR did not take any retaliatory measures against the economic sanctions imposed by the West in 1980.

The present political coolness between the USSR and Japan could retard the expansion of economic relations. Behind this lies the historical unpopularity of the Russians with the Japanese. Public opinion polls show that the USSR is always among the countries that the Japanese dislike the most.[14] No peace treaty between them has existed in the post-war period and the major hindrance to the conclusion of one is the territorial issue of the northern islands, an issue for which there is no prospect of a quick resolution. High-level dialogue between the two governments has been infrequent, especially after the Soviet invasion of Afghanistan in December 1979. This event intensified the Japanese fear of the 'Russian threat' to a considerable degree. These are psychological matters on the Japanese side, and to what extent they have affected or will effect a downward trend of trade is hard to say. The only thing that seems to be certain is that the conclusion of a peace treaty, of which there is virtually no chance in the near future, would bring about a 'Soviet trade boom' in the Japanese business community.

Another important political factor is the unique Japanese relationship with the United States. The United States is the most important partner for Japan both from the point of view of its national economy and of its foreign policy. So far as their economic relations alone are concerned, nearly a quarter of Japanese exports go to the United States and about one sixth of its imports come from that country. In 1981, for instance, the United States took 25.7 per cent of Japan's total exports, and provided 17.7 per cent of its total imports. Therefore, it may not be in Japan's best interests to have unlimited economic relations with the USSR without regard to its extensive overall reliance upon the United States. The Japanese government appears to be prepared to sacrifice trade relations with the USSR when this is required to maintain good relations with the United States. This posture of the Japanese government was clearly reflected in its economic measures against the USSR after the Soviet invasion of Afghanistan. The United States seems to be highly sensitive to the Japanese export of energy-related machinery and equipment to the USSR and to a possible increase in Japan's dependence upon the USSR for energy resources in future.[15] This US concern might discourage further Japanese cooperation with the USSR in the energy area at some stage in the coming decade. A sign of this has already been perceived in the fact that the progress of the Sakhalin oil and gas project was put in jeopardy by a new round of economic sanctions imposed on the USSR by the US government after the Polish crisis.[16] The sanctions were lifted on 13 November 1982.

Looking back at the trend of trade between the Soviet Union and Japan over the past one-and-a-half decades, it is clear that the emergence of Siberian collaborative projects functioned as a strong impetus to trade at large. The first wave of trade was the realization of the First-Stage Soviet Far East Forest Resources Development Project in 1968. Japanese exports within the framework of this project between 1969 and 1970 accounted for over 20 per cent of its total exports to the USSR and around 60 per cent of its machinery and equipment exports to the country. The second wave, which was much stronger than the first, came with the realization of large-scale projects between 1974 and 1976. Although the total sum of credit extended by Japan for these projects came to just 20 per cent of its total exports to the USSR in this period, the implications are greater than this statistic might suggest, for a substantial number of deals outside the projects were said to be expedited as a result of the numerous negotiations over the projects themselves.

In the light of these considerations, an examination of the prospects for Siberian collaborative projects has particular significance in evaluating future economic relations as a whole between the two states. There are number of economically fundamental problems which will decrease the likelihood of the realization of new collaborative projects in the next decade.

In the first place, there is a gap in geographical priorities between Japan and the USSR. In the current plan of Siberian development the USSR still lays emphasis on west Siberia, while Japan wants to obtain the natural resources east of Lake Baikal. For example, if the Japanese side proposes a project in the eastern part of Siberia, the Soviets would accept it only on condition that the Japanese bear a substantial portion of the total developing cost for the project. The Japanese would retort that this would not be fair because the development would in the long run be in the interests of the USSR. Quite a few proposed projects have been abandoned or suspended in this way.[17]

Second, in the case of collaborative projects, Japan is not allowed to export capital in the form of joint ventures. This means that the Japanese have to leave the Soviets in full charge of actual development, which takes a long time by Japanese standards.

Third, the natural resources in which Japan is interested are in most cases situated in untrodden and inaccessible areas. Therefore, prior to the actual development of the natural resources, a huge amount of investment is needed for improving the infrastructure of the area, such as building railways or roads. These costs are often incorporated into the Soviet proposal, which makes the project unfeasible for Japan.

Finally, the serious capital shortages in the Soviet economy will be the most immediate restraint on the realization of any new projects. Generally speaking, Soviet central planners seem to be forced to put a higher priority on old, half-done projects than on new, large-scale projects largely because of capital and labour shortages in the next decade.[18] Consequently there is little chance that the Soviet economy can afford to engage in any new, large-scale Japanese–Soviet Siberian projects in the near future.

An equally important economic factor is the static trade structure between the two countries. As is evident from Table 8.2, the trade structure has been stable to a considerable extent over the past two decades. Steel and machinery dominated Japanese exports, and major items of Soviet exports continued to be raw materials and mineral fuel. Such a trade structure reveals that their economic relations are based on complementary needs. However, the nature of the Japanese–Soviet trade structure is similar to a typical trade structure between a developed and a developing country.

Among Japanese exports in the 1970s, steel exports, in particular the export of large-diameter pipes for natural-gas pipeline systems, have emerged as a key item and have become as important as machinery exports. Steel is expected to continue to be a stable Japanese export item throughout the 1980s because Soviet technology in this field is not advanced enough to meet its large domestic demand for various kinds of steel.

So far as Japanese imports are concerned, the start of energy supplies (LNG, coking coal) from Siberia, within the framework of the current collaborative projects, will considerably increase the share of energy resources in total Japanese imports from the USSR. On the other hand, it is predictable that the USSR will intensify its demand to be allowed to supply the raw materials to Japan in a more developed and worked form, although the Japanese are generally reluctant to accede to this demand. This sort of request by the Soviets was already observed in the negotiations on the Forest Resources Project.[19] The USSR is also increasingly keen on promoting the sale of its industrial goods to Japan.

However, apart from primary goods, it is difficult to find any items that would be likely cases for export to Japan in the foreseeable future. The basic problem for the USSR is that it cannot produce industrial goods of the quality necessary to sell them in Japan. This is a common constraint on East–West trade as a whole[20] As a general rule, the magnitude of East–West trade largely depends upon how much hard currency is available for the East to buy Western goods, and how much hard currency is available to the East is primarily determined by two elements: the ability of Eastern countries to sell their goods to the West and the amount of credit they can obtain from international financial markets. However, as mentioned above, acquiring cheap credits from the West has become increasingly difficult for the East. Although the Soviet economic posture is unique in the East in the sense that it has vast natural resources in Siberia, the USSR is by no means free of these restraints. In fact, they hold true for Japanese–Soviet trade. This implies not only that the trade structure between them is quite unlikely to undergo a substantial change, as the USSR wishes, but also that the level of Japanese–Soviet trade has little chance of rising sharply in the coming decade.

Before proceeding to Sino–Soviet economic relations, it is necessary to raise a question related both to Japanese–Soviet and to Sino–Japanese economic relations. Can China be seen as an alternative to Siberia as a partner for Japan in energy projects? On the economic front of the triangular relationship between Japan, China and the USSR, while Sino–Soviet trade is meagre, as will be discussed in the next section, Japan is the most important trading partner in the Far East both for the USSR and for China, and for the same reason: namely, Japan provides the Western technology both need and at the same time offers a large export market for their natural resources.

Against this background the USSR might possibly fear that Japan would turn to Chinese oil and coal reserves and show no more interest in cooperation over Siberian development. It is noteworthy that Japanese political relations with China today are in marked contrast to its cool relations with the USSR. A peace treaty was signed between Japan and China in 1978, and the national feeling of Japan towards China is generally very good. In short, the political background is much more favourable to expanding economic relations between Japan and China than to collaboration between Japan and the USSR.

However, when one takes into account the considerable difference in the stage of economic development reached by the USSR and China, a simple comparison of the two states as Japanese trade partners or energy suppliers may be misleading. The basic nature of present Sino–Japanese economic relations has a strong element of economic aid, particularly in the case of projects and plant exports. On the other hand, Japanese–Soviet economic relations are based much more on commercial deals.

The fact is that China is still very much a backward country incapable of embarking upon large-scale collaborative projects for developing energy resources as a reciprocal trade partner with Japan. This means that the present economic situation of China may not permit it to become a substantial energy supplier for Japan in the near future. Given these factors, it is perhaps too early to view Japanese energy cooperation with China as an alternative to cooperation with the USSR, even if China has a large potential as an energy supplier to Japan.

Sino–Soviet economic relations

Although Sino–Soviet relations are quite a popular subject among Western historians and political scientists, the economic aspect of the relationship, since its deterioration from the late 1950s, has seldom been dealt with.

The level of Sino–Soviet trade continued to decline drastically throughout the 1960s after reaching a pinnacle in 1959, and recorded the lowest figure in modern times, US $46.6 million, in 1970. Nevertheless, despite the fact that no substantial improvement of political relations between the two states was seen in the 1970s, the turnover of trade gradually increased during the decade (see Table 8.3). The share of Sino–Soviet trade in the total volume of Soviet foreign trade was well below 0.5 per cent even at its highest level over the last decade. For the Chinese part, the quantity of trade with the USSR has not accounted for more than 3 per cent of its total foreign trade in most years of the 1970s. Although the volume of trade between them was not significant, it was not small enough to be totally disregarded. A certain level of trade relations has existed in spite of the severe political rivalry between the two states.

Turning to the trade structure, Table 8.4 clearly indicates that the major items among Soviet exports to China are machinery, equipment and transport materials. Above all, transport machinery such as lorries or air-transport facilities occupies the most important position among Soviet exports to China. As for Soviet imports from China, agricultural goods and textile products take large shares. In short, the trade structure again takes the form of trade between a developed country and a developing country. But in this case the USSR plays the role of a developed country. However, statistics for 1981 show that the level of

Table 8.3 *Soviet trade with China, Mongolia and the DPRK, 1970–81 (millions of US dollars)*

	1970	1971	1972	1973	1974	1975	1976	1977	1978	1979	1980	1981
China												
Turnover	46.6	154.1	254.1	273.4	282.7	278.0	417.0	337.2	495.6	507.3	487.2	245.6
Export	24.9	77.9	120.9	136.5	143.3	128.6	238.5	160.8	239.8	267.4	261.0	114.7
Import	21.7	76.2	133.2	136.9	139.4	149.4	178.5	176.4	255.8	239.9	226.2	130.8
Mongolia												
Turnover	256.5	261.4	346.4	459.8	534.3	665.9	815.2	918.4	1087.7	1177.5	1359.8	1438.8
Export	198.1	182.0	253.6	340.4	376.9	492.2	629.8	747.4	872.7	907.3	1040.8	1093.5
Import	58.4	79.4	92.8	119.4	157.4	173.7	185.4	171.0	215.0	270.2	319.0	345.3
DPRK												
Turnover	373.2	502.6	458.4	485.3	453.6	468.8	398.6	446.1	553.3	750.3	880.4	735.0
Export	230.0	366.8	303.5	304.2	256.8	258.9	241.2	223.7	258.4	359.3	443.1	387.4
Import	143.2	135.8	154.9	181.1	196.8	209.9	157.4	222.4	294.9	391.0	437.4	347.6

Source: *UN Year Book of International Trade Statistics*, Vol. 1.

trade between them fell to half of that of the previous year (Table 8.3). This was the result of a substantial fall in the volume of two-way trade in the traditionally important goods mentioned above. In particular, the drastic decrease of Soviet exports to China in 1981 is attributable to the sharp decline in its sales of lorries, air-transport facilities, and other transport materials, since the volume of its exports of other goods in 1981 remained much the same as in the previous year. Whether this sudden change in the trade pattern between the two states is just a temporary phenomenon or demonstrates the start of a new trend remains to be seen.

According to Chinese sources,[21] the settlement of trade between the two states is carried out in a manner very similar to barter. Data on the technical details of the method are not available. If there is a trade imbalance, the balance appears to be carried forward to the accounts of the next year, and transferable roubles are utilized for part of the payment. The same sources suggest that the USSR and China concluded a five-year trade and payment agreement in the mid-1970s. Before this agreement, they had signed an annual trade and payment agreement. The conclusion of such a long-term agreement may imply that both the USSR and China are committed to continuing trade relations in the future and recognize the merit of a longer-term framework.

Major reasons for the existence of constant, if not substantial, trade relations should be sought in the context of economic need. First, machinery and equipment made in the USSR are by and large considerably cheaper than those made in the West (although the quality of

Table 8.4 *Shift in percentage share of machinery, equipment and transport materials in total Soviet exports to China, Mongolia and the DPRK, 1970–81*

Year	China	Mongolia	DPRK
1970	60.6	54.9	43.2
1971	70.1	51.4	30.4
1972	75.7	55.2	38.1
1973	74.5	53.0	36.2
1974	74.3	58.8	43.2
1975	75.1	62.4	40.5
1976	68.3	66.5	27.5
1977	54.2	68.3	20.6
1978	58.5	69.4	15.1
1979	57.4	63.8	21.2
1980	58.0	65.1	28.5
1981	21.2	61.7	30.3

Source: Calculated from *Vneshnyaya torgovlya SSSR*, various years.

Soviet products is usually not as high as that of Western goods). This may be the chief advantage for China in purchasing Soviet industrial goods. Second, geographical proximity is always a positive element in trade relations between any two countries. In this respect, it is noteworthy that officials of the Soviet Ministry of Foreign Trade have a tendency to emphasize the merit of the geographical propinquity between the USSR and Japan in an attempt to strengthen economic links with Japan.[22]

Third, it must not be overlooked that Soviet economic ties with China in the 1950s were strong not only in terms of volume but also in terms of value. The USSR is supposed by the end of 1957 to have helped in the construction of all major industrial enterprises in China; to have provided industrial and technical blueprints for Chinese use; and to have supplied between 7,000 and 10,000 experts to China and to have trained an estimated 10,000 Chinese in the USSR.[23] Bearing in mind the magnitude of Soviet assistance in this period, it would be fair to assume that spare parts and affiliated materials for plants and equipment installed with Soviet aid in the 1950s still constitute a substantial share of current Chinese imports from the USSR. The list of Soviet export items to China contains many items termed 'accessories and spare parts'. In this context, it is interesting to note that after the cancellation of the Soviet–Egyptian treaty of friendship and cooperation in 1976, China and Egypt concluded an agreement for Chinese delivery of spare parts for Soviet weapons and other military equipment in Egypt.[24] Whether they are imported from the USSR and re-exported to Egypt or are produced in Chinese plants is hard to tell. In any case, this agreement proves that some spare parts for Soviet machinery and equipment are available in China even today.

Economics aside, it may not be unrealistic for the USSR to see some political significance in maintaining trade links with China. At the moment such links are one of the very few communication channels between them. However, the chances of the USSR being able to use trade links as a useful tool of policy vis-à-vis China are very slim. Imports of machinery and equipment from the USSR may still hold some importance in the Chinese economy. However, the general trend appears to be that China is trying to solidify economic ties with the West, particularly in key sectors of its economy, and to free its industries from Soviet influence. The non-communist share in China's trade rose to nearly 85 per cent by the mid-1970s – the largest share in any communist country's trade.[25] Under these circumstances, it is difficult to imagine a situation in which the USSR might find it feasible and effective to carry out economic sanctions against China in order to squeeze out of it major political concessions. On the other hand, massive Soviet economic assistance for the modernization of China in the expectation of achieving diplomatic gains is equally unlikely to take place. From the economic point of view alone, its economic capacity may not make this option available to the Soviet Union, which already has a long list of developing countries both inside and outside Comecon to which it gives a large amount of economic aid.

In sum, as long as their political relations remain as severe as in the past two decades, the degree of Sino–Soviet economic relations will continue to be too low to have any substantial impact on the non-economic aspects of their relations. Nevertheless, it remains possible that trade will increase as China seeks to demonstrate its equidistance between the superpowers.

Finally, we must refer briefly to the relationship of Siberian development to possible Sino–Soviet economic cooperation. Theoretically, provided political relations are favourable between China and the USSR, Siberian development and Sino–Soviet trade would accelerate each other. Developing Siberia would increase the demand for consumer goods made in China which are utilized by the Soviet workforce in Siberia, and at the same time natural resources developed there and industrial products manufactured in Siberian production complexes would go to the Chinese market. However, history has never witnessed such a situation in Siberia in the past, and there is very little prospect of seeing its emergence unless a major breakthrough on the political front takes place. The hard reality is that the chief Chinese concern at the moment, with regard to Siberia, seems to be the military implications of the area's development – as an intensified threat to its security – rather than the potential economic benefit of large-scale economic cooperation there with the USSR.

Mongolian–Soviet economic relations

No other state in the Far East can compare with Mongolia in terms of heavy economic dependency on the USSR. It may not be an exaggeration to say that there is not a single sector of the Mongolian economy that has been free of Soviet influence. Citing some statistical facts may suffice to show how much its economy has relied upon the USSR and how deeply the USSR has been involved in the economic development of Mongolia. The enterprises built in the country with Soviet technical and economic assistance as of early 1982 are claimed to turn out about 50 per cent of the total volume of its industrial output, including 90 per cent of electricity, about 80 per cent of coal, 90 per cent of flour and 100 per cent of copper–molybdenum concentrate.[26] The USSR accounts for over 80 per cent of Mongolia's total foreign trade. Imports from the USSR meet over 90 per cent of its domestic requirements for machinery and equipment; 100 per cent for oil, oil products and rolled ferrous; and 50 per cent for consumer goods.[27]

Soviet economic aid to Mongolia is enormous. Mongolia ranks top among Comecon beneficiaries of aid from the USSR. Michael Kaser points out that by 1 January 1980 the USSR had undertaken to build 621 enterprises or projects in Mongolia, and of these 389 were already being exploited. This means that for every $3\frac{1}{2}$ enterprises or projects built in Comecon countries, one was built in Mongolia.[28] According to his calculation, the USSR provided over 11 per cent of Mongolian GNP in 1976–9. Alan J. K. Sanders writes that 250 Soviet economic-aid projects in Mongolia were agreed for 1976–80, including 121 in agriculture, 17 in the fuel and power industry, 8 in mining and 22 in the light and food industries.[29]

A cosy and extensive economic relationship between the two states dates back to the early 1920s. The first trade agreement between them was signed in 1923, two years after Mongolia became Soviet Russia's first political ally after the former's revolution of 11 July 1921. In the mid-1920s the USSR played a decisive role in establishing Mongolia's monetary system. In December 1925 the *tugrik*, the first national currency in Mongolia, was put into circulation by a joint Mongolian–Soviet central bank, indicating the magnitude of the Soviet presence in the Mongolian economy in these years.

Mongolia's introduction of a state monopoly of trade in 1930 rendered the USSR virtually its sole trading partner, as other countries responded to the monopoly by breaking off trade relations with Mongolia.[30] In 1934, some new agreements were concluded between them, including arrangements for the settlement of mutual accounts and for joint stock companies. The USSR continued to be Mongolia's dominant economic partner throughout the Second World War, and in 1946 a new agreement on economic and cultural cooperation was signed together with a treaty of friendship and mutual assistance. In 1949 the first long-term trade agreement, covering a five-year period (1950–4), was signed following Mongolia's introduction of its first five-year plan (1948–52). In 1954 and 1957 the two states signed their second and third long-term trade agreements, each covering a three-year period (1955–7, 1958–60). These were followed by long-term agreements covering five-year periods (1961–5, 1966–70, 1971–5, 1976–80, 1981–5). The most recent was signed in October 1980 in Moscow.

As far as Mongolian–Soviet economic relations are concerned, ordinary foreign trade merely represents one aspect, for their economic ties have developed to an extent that is far beyond normal commercial trade relations. In this respect, it is worth noting that Mongolian officials concerned with the economy have in recent years tended to emphasize what they term 'direct contacts' or 'direct business cooperation' between ministries of the two governments. It is reported that in 1975 a Mongolian Politburo member disclosed that 'direct contact' had been established between 13 ministries and departments in Mongolia and 20 in the USSR, and that 40 Mongolian research institutes had 'business contacts' with over 80 Soviet scientific establishments.[31] The counsellor for economic affairs at the Mongolian embassy in the USSR, Magsaryn Chimiddorzh, explained the setting-up of joint Mongolian–Soviet economic associations and the establishment of direct, interministry contacts with the USSR as the outcome of improved and diversified economic relations between the two countries, and claimed that such direct contacts would be extended further in future.[32]

One of the most typical examples of direct contacts and cooperation may be the joint project for a copper and molybdenum mining and concentrating complex at Erdenent, in the northern part of Mongolia. This agreement, the largest industrial project in the history of the Mongolian economy, was concluded between the two governments in 1973, and the third stage of the project was completed in 1981. Mongolsovtsvetmet, the Mongolian–Soviet joint stock company for mining non-ferrous metals, established in the same year, is supposed to have played the central role in the financial aspects of this project. It would be interesting to compare the features of the Erdenent project with Japan–Soviet Siberian development projects, and some similarities between them can be identified. The USSR grants Mongolia credit on favourable terms, by which Mongolia purchases required machinery and equipment for the project. The Mongolians in return repay the credit by deliveries of Erdenent products after the project starts operation. This kind of arrangement is also seen in Japanese–Soviet projects, albeit the Soviet position is the opposite of that in the Erdenent project. Its position is also markedly different from Japan's position in Siberian projects in that the USSR not only holds an equal share of capital in the Erdenent project with Mongolia, but is also sending Soviet personnel to supervise and guide the construction. It is also known that Mongolian workers for the complex are being trained in the USSR.[33] All these factors show that the Soviet role in the Erdenent project is much more direct and dominant than Japan's role in Siberian collaborative projects, reflecting the nature of economic relations between the USSR and Mongolia.

It would be fair to argue that Mongolian–Soviet economic relations are very political. Although their geographical contiguity justifies their close economic links to some extent, the current degree of Mongolia's trade dependency on the USSR is by no means normal, and the amount of Soviet economic aid to the country is huge by any standard. Moreover, the manner of Soviet direct intervention in the domestic economic affairs of Mongolia is certainly unusual in a relationship between two independent countries. Mongolia became a member of Comecon in 1962, and both the USSR and Mongolia often stress that their economic cooperation has come to be all the more effective and advantageous within the framework of Comecon. Nevertheless, the fact remains that their special economic ties had developed well before Mongolia's affiliation to Comecon rather than as a result of its membership.

The unique economic relations between the two countries should be put into the perspective of overall Soviet foreign policy in the Far East. From the political and strategic points of view, the USSR vitally needs to keep Mongolia as a close ally and to continue to deter the country from turning to China by maintaining extraordinarily close economic ties with it. It may be obvious that the Mongolian economy would collapse the moment the USSR broke off economic links with the country. In this sense the USSR may retain a strong leverage on Mongolia. The room for the USSR to employ it, however, would be very limited. It would be possible for Mongolia, just like the DPRK, to attempt to play off the USSR against China in the hope of drawing economic aid from both states if the USSR were to threaten to change policies towards Mongolia. Any major change in Soviet economic policies towards Mongolia seems, therefore, quite unlikely in the foreseeable future. Most probably the USSR will pour an exceptionally high level of economic aid into Mongolia and 'direct contacts' between the two national economies will further intensify in the next decade.

When it comes to the prospect for trade turnover, however, the situation appears to be different. Although Soviet exports to Mongolia showed relatively favourable growth over the last decade, its imports from Mongolia were largely stagnant (see Table 8.3). Bearing in mind that the main items among Mongolian exports to the USSR have remained primary goods like meat, wool and cattle, sharp increases in these exports in the next decade cannot be expected. Taking this and the mounting trade deficit on the Mongolian side into consideration, the poor Mongolian export capability may check the increase in volume of two-way Mongolian–Soviet trade in the coming decade.

Korean–Soviet economic relations

Some of the features of economic relations between the DPRK and the USSR appear to be common with those of Mongolian–Soviet relations. Korean–Soviet trade has also been conducted on a long-term basis, and five-year trade agreements have been concluded every five years since 1960. The latest one was signed in Pyongyang in 1981. Close contacts between the two governments or concerned organizations have also taken place. In 1967 an intergovernmental consultative commission on economic, scientific and technological problems was founded in an attempt to explore possibilities of utilizing new, more effective forms of cooperation. It is claimed that direct contacts have been stepped up in recent years between the State Planning Committee of the USSR and its counterpart in the DPRK.[34] Compensation-based cooperation with the USSR, typically seen in the Erdenent project, is supposed to have recently become widespread in the DPRK as well.

Soviet economic and technical aid in the main industrial sectors is again one of the central elements in economic relations between the DPRK and the USSR. By 1980 some 59 industrial projects in total are claimed to have been built or retooled in the country with Soviet economic and technical aid.[35] They included the country's largest thermal-power station in Pukchong, the Musan iron-ore mine, coal-mines in Anju, Kim Chak iron-and-steel plant, the Pyongyang motor-battery plant, and the Pyongyang cargo railway terminal. According to Soviet estimates, these projects built with Soviet assistance account for about 60 per cent of the total national output of electricity, 30 per cent of steel, 34 per cent of rolled metal, 45 per cent of oil products, 20 per cent of fabrics and 40 per cent of iron ore.[36]

The USSR is definitely the DPRK's main trading partner, accounting for about a third of its total foreign trade.[37] Traditionally the USSR has supplied machinery and equipment to the DPRK for its key industries. For Korea's part, the main items among its exports to the USSR are raw materials, food and textile goods. The above illustrations may demonstrate the similarities in the patterns of Korean–Soviet and Mongolian–Soviet economic relations.

It must be stressed, however, that Korean economic links with the USSR over the past decade have been much less firm[38] and the Soviet command of and presence in the Korean economy are less than in the Mongolian case. Despite the boastful claim by the USSR about its contribution to the industrialization of the DPRK, the last decade did not show a substantial growth of trade between them. On the contrary, after turnover reached a peak in 1971 the general trend was downwards until 1976, although a modest recovery was seen over the last few years (see Table 8.3). A more significant point may be that the share of machinery and equipment in the total export of the USSR to the DPRK substantially declined in the second half of the 1970s. This share shrank to just about 20 per cent at the end of the 1970s, less than half that of the mid-1970s (see Table 8.4). Bearing in mind that the amount of Soviet exports to the country was stable during the decade, this declining share means a decrease in the volume of machinery and equipment exports in absolute terms.

Whether or not this change in the pattern of Soviet exports in the latter half of the 1970s indicates a change in its trade policy towards the DPRK remains to be seen. The fact that the share of machinery and equipment exports started to rise again in 1979 makes the implication more vague and complicated. It seems possible that the change had some relation to a renewed deterioration of the political relationship between the two states which was made overt by the failure of the North Korean Party chief, Kim Il-sung, to visit Moscow during his tour of communist states in 1975.[39] Among other factors was a substantial cut-down of the Soviet supply of military hardware to the DPRK.[40] The fact that very few articles on Soviet economic cooperation with the DPRK have appeared in recent years in the official Soviet periodical *Foreign Trade*, issued by the Ministry of Foreign Trade, might imply that Soviet economic assistance towards the DPRK is fairly low-key. The gap between the degree of Soviet economic commitment to Mongolia and to the DPRK should be considered as a political product, reflecting the difference between the political positions in the Far East of these two smaller communist states and the difference in the priorities accorded to them in Soviet foreign policy.

Apart from politics, given the critical financial situation of the DPRK, which was disclosed by international defaults in 1977, including huge debts owed to the USSR,[41] the prospect of a favourable growth of trade with the USSR in the coming decade seems slight. However, this is not to say that the USSR has no economic leverage on the DPRK. It seems that in the last decade the USSR sought to use trade as a political weapon vis-à-vis the DPRK, albeit not in an extreme way.[42] However, performance was poor, and the only major consequence seems to be closer trade links between the DPRK and China and Japan. It may be true that the large quantity of oil supplied by the USSR to the DPRK is essential to the Korean economy. Nevertheless any attempt to apply political pressure to the DPRK by threatening to stop oil supplies would be perilous for the USSR. It could drive the DPRK towards China which, in the Soviet eyes, might be detrimental to the national security of the USSR in the Far East.

Therefore, provided that the Soviet policy of minimizing the importance of Korean affairs continues to be its basic stance towards the DPRK, and provided the DPRK continues to balance China and the USSR carefully in the diplomatic realm, it is unlikely that any drastic change in the magnitude of economic ties between the DPRK and the USSR will take place in the foreseeable future.

Conclusion

The picture drawn in this chapter of Soviet economic relationships with states in the Far East stresses the dissimilarities in the features and patterns of each of these relationships. Political elements seem to have been predominant in the USSR's economic links with Mongolia and the DPRK. That has been revealed in the form of large-scale and direct economic assistance in many key sectors of their national economies, although the magnitude of the impact on the two countries was very different. It cannot be denied that such economic ties mean liabilities for the USSR. However, the USSR would appear to accept its massive economic aid to Mongolia, and to a lesser extent to the DPRK, as an economic cost of its political objectives in the Far East. Therefore, most probably the USSR will increase, if not willingly, its economic aid to Mongolia. It has in fact already pledged to double it during the first half of the 1980s.[43] Although the USSR's economic commitment to the DPRK seems not to be as strong as to Mongolia, it would not be able drastically to downgrade economic ties with the DPRK out of political considerations. As for Sino–Soviet trade relations, to what extent political elements have affected them is a matter of judgement. It may be safe to contend that the continuance of the current modest volume of trade between them is mainly an economic consequence of their geographical proximity and the legacy of their close economic ties in the 1950s.

Japanese–Soviet economic relationships are not independent of politics either. Nevertheless the negative political factors discussed in this paper can in principle be perceived as potential problems rather than direct obstacles to their economic relations. Restrictions on the transfer of Western technology to the USSR, especially in energy areas, the initiative for which is always taken by the United States, would dash some trade deals between them in the next decade. However, even when economic sanctions were imposed on the USSR after the invasion of Afghanistan, the Japanese government did not prevent actual trade deals in a direct way, and the outcome was that the turnover of Japanese–Soviet trade in 1980 showed a modest growth (see Table 8.1). My view is that although politics may be felt from time to time, the long-term trend of economic relations between the two states will be determined primarily by economic factors, as in the past. Above all, long-term economic need and more importantly the capability of the USSR to buy Japanese industrial products which contain Western technology would be a decisive variable in the future trend. This is also the case with Japan–Soviet Siberian development projects. Therefore, even if all political problems are removed, the unlimited expansion of economic relations between the two states would not be possible, no matter how large the potential for Siberian cooperation may be.

Despite all these dissimilar conditions, it may be possible to draw some general conclusions on the future prospects of Soviet economic relations with the states in the Far East. For one thing, it appears to be unlikely that the magnitude of trade between the USSR and these countries will grow sharply in the next decade. Nevertheless, it remains true that trade with Japan will have a predominant position in the Soviet economy since trade with that country seems already to be embedded in its national economy. For another, the scope for the USSR to gain any major political points by means of economic leverage in the Far East appears to be very limited. In this respect, the DPRK may perhaps be the only state in the Far East on which the USSR could exercise economic leverage to some extent; but to do so to any great extent would also create a serious setback in Soviet foreign policies towards the DPRK and China. In sum, the need to maintain economic links with Japan for the sake of its own national economy, the low level of Sino–Soviet trade, the importance of Mongolia's impregnable loyalty and the risk of the DPRK's political inconstancy makes it unlikely that the USSR will use economic policy as an effective foreign-policy tool.

Notes

[1] For background material, see Wolfgang Berner (ed.), *The Soviet Union 1975–76* (London, Hurst, 1977), p. 274.

[2] Kazuo Ogawa, *Nisso Boeki no Jitsujo to Kadai* (The actual state and problems of Japanese–Soviet trade) (Tokyo, Kyoikusha, 1979), p. 23.

[3] See, for example, Gunnar Adler-Karlsson, *Western Economic Warfare 1947–1967* (Stockholm, Almquist & Wiksell, 1968).

[4] K. Ogawa, *Nisso Jitsujo to Kadai*, p. 25.

[5] D. V. Petrov, *Soren Kara Mita Nippon* (Japan in the eyes of the Soviet Union) (Tokyo, Simul Press, 1975), p. 173–6.

[6] The sum of bank loans extended to the USSR by the EXIM Bank between 1974 and 1977 amounted to US $3.4 billion, including the loan for Siberian collaborative projects.

[7] The ninth session of the joint conference has not yet been held, as of September 1982.

[8] A bank loan to the USSR of up to about US $1 billion was committed by the EXIM Bank for this project in December 1980.

[9] The USSR put forward some tentative ideas of future possible projects at the fourth executive session of the joint conference between the two committees in February 1979, but no further detailed explanation of them has yet been given to the Japanese, as of September 1982.

[10] Speech at the Japanese–American bilateral conference in Shimoda, Japan, September 1981.

[11] Unpublished material of the Japanese Defense Agency.

[12] Allen S. Whiting, *Siberian Development and East Asia: The Strategic Dimension* (Washington, DC, Association of American Geographers, 1980), p. 30.

[13] For example, at the Japanese–Soviet Symposium sponsored by Sankei in Sapporo, Japan, November 1981, a Soviet representative of the Ministry of Foreign Trade contended that the economic sanctions against the USSR imposed by the Japanese government greatly undermined the trading partnership between the two states.

[14] See, for example, Hayao Shimizu, *Nipponjin wa Naze Sorenga Kiraika?* (Why do the Japanese dislike the Soviet Union?) (Tokyo, Yamanote Shyobo, 1979), p. 24.

[15] See, for example, the report of the Office of Technology Assessment

(OTA), US Congress, 'Technology and Soviet energy availability' (Washington, DC, November 1981).

[16] In June 1982, the US government imposed a ban on the export of products made with the use of US technology in Europe and Japan.

[17] Interview with Mr Keisuke Suzuki, chief researcher of the Japan–Soviet Business Cooperation Committee, in Tokyo, July 1981.

[18] Keisuke Suzuki, *Shiberia Kaihatsu to Nisso Keisai Kyoryoku* (Siberian development and Japanese–Soviet economic cooperation) (Tokyo, Nikkan Kogyo, 1977), pp. 203–7.

[19] It is reported that negotiations on the Third-Stage Forest Resources Project were prolonged partly because the Soviet side stuck to its demand for an increased share of timber delivery instead of lumber.

[20] Alec Nove, *East–West Trade: Problems, Prospects, Issues* (Beverley Hills, California, Sage Publications, 1978), pp. 34, 43.

[21] Interview with a Chinese economist from the Institute of World Economy, Chinese Academy of Social Science, in Oxford, August 1982.

[22] For example, speech by a Soviet representative at the Sankei Japanese–Soviet Symposium, November 1981.

[23] Colin Bown and Peter J. Mooney, *Cold War to Détente 1945–80* (London, Heinemann, 1981), p. 117.

[24] W. Berner (ed.), *The Soviet Union 1975–76*, p. 219.

[25] Ramon H. Myers, *The Chinese Economy Past and Present* (Belmont, Calif. Wadsworth, 1980), p. 247.

[26] Magsaryn Chimiddorzh, 'Mongolian–Soviet cooperation: some results and prospects', *Foreign Trade* (Moscow), February 1982.

[27] Jondongiyn Ochir, 'Mongolia–USSR: 60 years of cooperation', ibid., July 1981.

[28] Michael Kaser, 'The industrial revolution in Mongolia', *The World Today*, January 1982.

[29] Alan J. K. Sanders, 'Mongolia 1975: "One crew in battle, one brigade in labour" with the USSR', *Asian Survey*, vol. 16, no. 1 (January 1976), p. 66.

[30] Jondongyin Ochir, 'Fifty-five years of the first Mongolian–Soviet trade agreement', *Foreign Trade* (Moscow), December 1978.

[31] A.J.K. Sanders, 'Mongolia 1975', p. 68.

[32] M. Chimiddorzh, 'Mongolian–Soviet cooperation', p. 25.

[33] Burenzhargalyn Avirmid, 'Erdenet – a joint project of Mongolia and the USSR', *Foreign Trade* (Moscow), March 1980.

[34] V. Andreyev and V. Osipov, 'Relations of the USSR and the European socialist countries with the DPRK in the 1970s', *Far Eastern Affairs* (Moscow), no. 1 (1982).

[35] B. Mikailov, '35 years of Soviet–Korean cooperation', ibid., no. 4 (1980).

[36] V. Moiseyev and N. Shubnikov, 'Sixth Congress of the Workers' Party of Korea: results and perspectives', ibid., no. 2 (1981).

[37] V. Andreyev and V. Osipov, 'Relations with the DPRK in the 1970s', p. 55.

[38] Donald S. Zagoria, 'Korea's future: Moscow's perspective', *Asian Survey*, vol. 17, no. 11 (November 1977).

[39] W. Berner (ed.), *The Soviet Union 1975–76*, p. 273.

[40] D. Zagoria, 'Korea's future', p. 1106.

[41] Ibid.
[42] Ibid.
[43] M. Chimiddorzh, 'Mongolian–Soviet cooperation', p. 25.

9 Soviet Policy in East Asia: The Certainty of Uncertainty
Gerald Segal

It would be very convenient to be able to suggest that there is a clear-cut pattern of Soviet policy in east Asia. But the only certainty in Moscow's policies in east Asia is that there are no certainties. Analysts elsewhere have offered clear answers to the question of whether the Soviet Union is more threatening than threatened, or more prudent than paranoid, in its east Asian policies. But the problem is more complex. The Soviet Union is both a power in Asia and the border of Europe in Asia. As a result, confusing and conflicting priorities in Soviet policy pose dilemmas and predicaments of power rather than certainties of policy. What are the essential problems faced by the Soviet Union in east Asia, and how does Moscow try to cope with them?

Power in Asia, but not an Asian power
In geographic terms it is absurd to argue that the Soviet Union is not an Asian power. With one-third of its vast territory lying east of Irkutsk in east Asian Siberia[1] the Soviet Union is the second largest Asian power (11 per cent smaller than China). But geographic and demographic facts suggest different conclusions. In that vast territory there is a population of less than 12 million, or 5 per cent of the Soviet Union's total. What is more, the authorities seem to have great problems in keeping that number from falling. Despite impressive government enticements, many people take the first opportunity to move to the European part of the Soviet Union.

Not only do the inhabitants of the Soviet Union tend not to see their country as a true Asian power, but it seems that other Asian states also share that view. The history of the expansion of Tsarist/Soviet power to east Asia is essentially a feature of the recent past (150 years) and there is little sign that the present Soviet power has always been accepted as an immutable fact. There have been too many shifting national boundaries and territorial realignments in the area of Soviet east Asia to have much confidence in the permanence of present borders. While it is difficult to suggest that Soviet power in the area is fragile, it is more plausible to suggest that in the popular consciousness of Asians, the Soviet Union is not an Asian power of long standing.

In order for the Soviet Union to be accepted as more of an Asian power, there will first have to be certain crucial changes in Moscow's perceptions of the area. It is true that the relative Soviet neglect of east Asian Siberia has been partly reversed in recent years, but the tasks that lie ahead are enormous. At the risk of tedious recapitulation, it should nevertheless be stressed that there are good reasons for the Soviet Union to see its east Asian territories as less than a pressing priority. In a state that already finds itself seriously pressed for development funds, the formidable tasks in the Asian region no doubt make Soviet planners willing to move slowly on the Siberian question.

East Asian Siberia's vast territory is riddled with problems for the would-be developer. The unforgiving climate is harsh even by Soviet standards. Hard permafrost not only makes agriculture a forbidding task, but also adds to the cost of industrial development and exploitation of natural wealth. But it would be a mistake to suggest that such problems render the area a quagmire suitable only for depositing dissidents. These negative points are stressed only because there has also been an opposite tendency among some analysts to suggest that east Asian Siberia is the bonanza of the future for the Soviet Union.

It is undoubtedly true that there are vast natural resources in this area. Minerals of various sorts, especially gold, have conjured up these bonanza images. Coupled with evidently important deposits of oil, gas and coal, the region is also said to offer long-term hopes for energy projects. In order to help develop this new frontier, the optimists point to the new railway (the Baikal–Amur, or BAM) being laid parallel to the Trans-Siberian Railway at great cost in money and men.

One can hardly argue that the Soviet Union can be optimistic about many aspects of its east Asian territory, but neither the bonanza nor the quagmire image is entirely correct. In short, there are both great prospects and great problems in the region. There is considerable incentive for the Soviet Union to expand and develop its east Asian holdings, but there are also good reasons why such development will be slow and costly.

Apart from geographic facts, it is military power that makes the Soviet Union a power in Asia. But once again it is evident that the extension of Soviet power is relatively new, and it is not entirely clear what purposes that power serves. There has been an obvious extension of Soviet military force eastwards, especially since the mid-1960s along the Sino–Soviet frontier. Furthermore, Soviet naval power in the Pacific has made important progress in the past decade. But as with most problems in strategic analysis, the deployment of capabilities does not necessarily explain the intentions for their use.

At present, both land and naval forces seem to be more prudent than paranoid and more for immunization than imperialism. There is undoubted Soviet power deployed in Asia, but then the military problems envisaged are wide-ranging and difficult. The superior quantity of Chinese forces is matched by superior Soviet quality. But neither power can claim anything like an overwhelming offensive potential. Soviet naval power is greater than that of the United States in all categories, but then east Asia is more crucial to Soviet security, and the United States is not the only potential enemy in the region.

Thus the Soviet Union is a power in Asia, but seems unwilling to make any great sacrifices to become a truly Asian power. So long as fundamental security and cultural/historical interests are seen to lie in the West, this assessment is unlikely to change. Soviet power in Asia will of course remain, but it is unlikely to increase in any dramatic way. This basic problem of national identity is also encouraged by the second major problem for the Soviet Union in Asia: the complexity of regional and international politics. Perhaps precisely because the Soviet Union is a relative newcomer to Asia, it finds these complexities even harder to handle.

The complexities of power

It may be a truism to say that multilateral international relations are complex, but that does not necessarily diminish the importance of the observation. It is true that the Soviet Union faces numerous other complex international problems, but few seem as intricate as the web of east Asian politics. Previous analysts have pointed to ambiguities in Soviet foreign policy in other parts of the world, but little attention has so far been paid to Soviet policy in east Asia. It seems apparent that the complexity of power in east Asia has been a crucial reason for Moscow's inability to evolve a coherent strategic view of the area.

The predicaments of power for the Soviet Union ensue primarily from the presence in the area of its superpower rival (the United States), its major land threat (China), as well as the premier economic power of Asia (Japan). Comparisons to other parts of the world are always dangerous, but suffice it to say that in the West, the Soviet Union has a relatively more simple configuration of power to face. In east Asia there are also two other, minor, communist states.

One, Mongolia, is more docile than almost any in Eastern Europe, and the other, Korea, is less docile than almost any in Eastern Europe. A brief review of some of the problems encountered by the Soviet Union in east Asia will substantiate the point that Moscow is unable to formulate an over-arching strategy for the area.

Take for example Soviet–Mongolian relations. The primary bond in that at times symbiotic relationship is a shared concern with Chinese power. Thus Moscow found that it could strengthen ties with the Mongols by playing up the China threat, but at the same time this policy harmed the more crucial need for détente in Sino–Soviet relations. Similarly, when economic links between China and Mongolia were cut back in line with the growing Sino–Soviet rift, it was Moscow that had to bear the main burden of the deterioration in the Mongolian economy. In the sphere of cultural politics, the Soviet Union is wary of playing up ethnic problems of Mongols in China, while supporting Mongolia's anti-China line, for fear of the issue affecting the federal Soviet Union's own Mongol population.

Soviet–Korean relations are even more complicated than the relatively simple Soviet–Mongolian ties. In the case of the DPRK, the problems are particularly intense because of the more direct involvement of the great powers in the unresolved Korean question. The Soviet Union found the problems so complex that it found it easier to assume a much lower profile in the DPRK and thereby avoid the worst of the problems. For example, support for the speedy reunification of Korea might undercut Chinese power in Pyongyang and indeed might be part of a rapprochement with China, but it would have serious repercussions on Soviet–Japanese ties and would probably bring a more forthright US involvement in the peninsula. On the other hand, if the Soviet Union tried to reduce even further its aid and comfort to the North Koreans, there might be a marginal improvement in relations with Japan and the United States, but China would only make gains in Pyongyang and the Soviet Union would lose even more control over events in the area. There are no simple solutions to the predicaments of power in Korea.

Soviet–Japanese relations are perhaps more simple than Soviet–Korean ties, but once again there is little room for manoeuvre for Moscow. Especially in an era of hardline US policies regarding economic deals with the Soviet Union, the Japanese find they can barely engage in any meaningful economic relations with Moscow. Much like the problems faced by the Kremlin in trying to entice West Europeans away from the US alliance, the Soviet Union finds that there are strict limits to what is possible. To be sure there are grounds for disagreement between the United States and its allies, but by and large Soviet efforts to pry them apart even further are ham-handed and in the end counterproductive. Moscow may toy with these minor policy options, but until it makes any major concessions on the disputed islands, or there is a major change in East–West relations, the Soviet Union has little room for manoeuvre in relations with Japan.

Sino–Soviet relations offer perhaps the greatest predicaments for Soviet policy-makers. They have found that a deterioration in Sino–

Soviet relations may have helped reinforce unity with Mongolia, and for a time helped improve relations with the United States and Japan, but in the long term, hostility to China seems to be very costly. Soviet leaders have struggled for 20 years with the problem of improving relations with China, but little has happened to promote a major breakthrough. Moscow has found that it cannot avoid dealing with China and the present hostility in relations only complicates the predicaments of power.

Finally there are Soviet–American relations. This bilateral relationship has really changed very little since 1945. What is perhaps most clear to the Soviet Union is that US power will not leave the Pacific region, and the link with Japan in particular is as strong as ever. The Kremlin has found that any change in Soviet–American relations in east Asia is fundamentally tied to broader superpower relations. This seems to suit the Soviet Union, for it too prefers to focus on the more crucial superpower level and the European balance. The complexities of power in east Asia have not been ones that the Soviet Union has been able to overcome, other than by minimizing the importance of the region and its problems, and concentrating on other more pressing problems.

Even though the Soviet Union is unable to act forthrightly because of the predicaments of power, and its lack of an overwhelming desire to become an Asian power, this is not to say that there will be no change in Soviet policy. Certainly there are numerous possibilities for change, and indeed several hypothetical patterns seem more crucial than others for the future.

The Mongolian model
Some have suggested that Soviet policy in Afghanistan and/or Kampuchea is part of an attempt to impose a Mongolian model on Soviet allies. It is suggested that the overwhelming dominance maintained by the Soviet Union in Mongolia is not only desired by the Kremlin, but also seen as obtainable in other states. There are of course serious problems with this theory, not only because the Afghan and Kampuchean cases are different from Mongolia in crucial strategic and political ways, but also because the Mongolian model is complex, and one that does not seem to hold much hope of being implemented outside Mongolia. Political control of Mongolia is maintained by the Soviet Union in a way that it is not able to do in perhaps any other state. The dominance of organizational links by Soviet officials is perhaps easier to achieve in Mongolia than elsewhere because of its tiny population. The result is an impressive degree of Soviet dominance, and it is not surprising that Mongolian foreign policy is also heavily dominated by the Soviet Union.

In many respects there are strong historical reasons for Soviet control of Mongolian policy.² At least in the past 150 years, Russian/Soviet power has been dominant. At times the Japanese and especially the Chinese have been important powers in the area, but the dominant trend seems to have been to blur the Mongolian–Soviet border and sharpen the line separating Mongolia from China. This trend continues to this day, and indeed is intensified by Mongolian fears of China's vast population and potential power. This is not to suggest that there is no concern on the part of the Mongolians with being swallowed by their neighbour to the north instead of their southern neighbour, but it seems that China continues to be seen as the more crucial threat. Thus, at its roots, Soviet political power in Mongolia appears overwhelming, and long-lasting.

Such strong political control can be modified in important ways. Mongolia's pro-Soviet orientation can be maintained while engaging in at least a modicum of détente with China. There are clear signs in recent years that some improvement of Sino–Mongolian ties, with Soviet approval, is in fact under way. In the first place there is the Soviet desire to lessen tension with China. Thus it is only natural that if Soviet policy should change, Mongolia's would be likely to move in step. Second, and more important, in 1982 the Chinese and Mongolians began meeting to discuss territorial problems arising from the 1964 border protocol.³ Given the sensitivity of frontier issues for both the Soviet Union and Mongolia, the meeting indicates serious intent to ease at least some of the tension in relations with China. This is not to say that Mongolia is drifting out of the Soviet orbit, but it does show that Mongolia's pro-Sovietism need not stem entirely from anti-Chinese motives.

Economically, Soviet control in Mongolia appears even more comprehensive.⁴ The organizational links marking the lines of Soviet power are not only bilateral, they also run through Comecon. It is striking that Mongolian five-year plans need to await agreement on the wider Comecon plans, and for an economy as small as Mongolia's, the impact of Comecon decisions is magnified. But the bilateral economic link with the Soviet Union still remains more crucial. Not only is Mongolia heavily in debt to the Soviet Union at present, but this trend is one of long standing. Economic dependence is of course not entirely satisfactory to the Soviet Union, especially if it should mean added strains on an already shaky Soviet economy.

In the mid-1970s the Erdenent development project near the Soviet frontier became the major symbol of bilateral economic ties. Apparently in an attempt to reduce the economic burden of Mongolia on the Soviet Union, the mineral resources of Erdenent were exploited, almost entirely for export to the Soviet Union. Thus the impact on the Mongolian economy of this major project is much smaller than might have been expected, but it also suggests a neocolonial, or more graciously a symbiotic, relationship between Mongolia and the Soviet Union. Erdenent is also a symbol of the attempt to blur the political lines between Mongolia and the Soviet Union, while keeping a firm Mongolian–China line. In sum, the Mongolian economic model has some problems for Soviet policy, but by and large is favourable to Soviet interests. But it should also be clear that the Mongolian model is heavily dependent on Mongolian conditions, and these appear to have limited applicability to other areas.

In the military sphere, the Mongolian model is perhaps the one most dominated by Soviet control. Especially since the outbreak of Sino–Soviet clashes along the frontier, Mongolia has been well integrated into the Soviet military area. Prior to the late 1960s there were already powerful organizational links which left the defence of Mongolia essentially to Soviet power. In the 1970s and after, this pattern of dependence has deepened, with Mongolia rendered little more than a component of the Transbaikal and far eastern military districts of the Soviet Union. The number of Soviet troops stationed in Mongolia is a greater percentage of the population than in any other state bound by a defence pact with the Soviet Union. This is not to suggest that the Soviet troops are deployed without the consent of the Mongolians. As has already been suggested in the discussion of political and economic relations, the symbiotic relationship suggests a shared concern with Chinese power. In this sense, Soviet defence is Mongolian defence.

This symbiosis need not rest on unalterably anti-China supports. While it is clear that the Soviet Union does not see its forces in Mongolia, or along the Sino–Soviet border in general, as being offensive, it is clear that some steps can be taken to reduce tensions by engaging in confidence-building measures. Even cosmetic troop-withdrawals or mutual presence at troop manoeuvres might be acceptable to both China and the Soviet Union, and would also not upset the Mongolians. But in the end there can be little significant change of military force in Mongolia. The Soviet Union has only Mongolia as a defensive glacis in the east, whereas it has a far more comprehensive system in the west. The removal of this glacis, as small as it is, would make Soviet defence-planners feel even more exposed along a lengthy and underpopulated Sino–Soviet frontier. In sum, in the military dimension, the Mongolian model is especially close to Soviet desires, but as with other aspects of Soviet–Mongolian ties, it is a case that seems applicable only to Mongolian conditions.

There can be little doubt that the Mongolian model is one that the Soviet Union would dearly like to see implemented elsewhere in east Asia. There may be certain difficulties, for example over economic dependence, but by and large the Soviet Union can be pleased about Mongolian 'symbiosis' in a way that it cannot with other Comecon partners. It is equally clear, however, that this docility on the part of Mongolia has little application elsewhere in east Asia. The Mongolian model can only be a model for Mongolia, and while the Soviet Union seems happy to retain the relationship as it is, there is little hope that it can be extended. Mongolia is an exception – albeit a positive exception – and Moscow acknowledges that it will not be the rule for its relations with other states. But if Soviet–Mongolian relations are not the model, what of other border states, like Korea?

The Korean model

Soviet relations with the DPRK do not provide a model for Soviet relations with east Asia so much as a mirror. The complexities and predicaments of power faced by Moscow seem to have been played out in microcosm in Soviet–Korean relations since 1945. More than any other bilateral relationship, Soviet–Korean ties are perhaps the best guide to Soviet policy in east Asia.

In the political sphere North Korea began as an even closer ally of the Soviet Union than Mongolia. But the removal of Soviet troops in the late 1940s and the Korean War, which brought Chinese power to greater prominence, meant a loosening of Soviet–Korean ties. In contrast with the Mongolian case, Moscow could not evict Chinese power as the Sino–Soviet split grew more serious. Faced also with problems resulting from Soviet–Japanese and Soviet–American relations, the Soviet Union set the pattern of its overall relations with east Asia and withdrew from active involvement. The 1940s and 1950s were periods of relative success in Soviet policy in Korea and east Asia, but the decades afterwards were distinctly more frustrating.

The Soviet Union did not withdraw entirely from Korean or east Asian affairs, but it did learn to live with less direct political power. The low-key policy of tolerating a semi-hostile China, or of coping with crisis management with the United States, meant the Soviet Union kept its finger in Korean and east Asian politics, but was unwilling to commit a limb and certainly not its entire body weight. What has emerged is not so much a model of the kind of political relations the Soviet Union desires in the area, but more a model based on a realistic appreciation of what can be achieved given the difficult political conditions. Clearly the Soviet Union would like better political relations with Korea, along Mongolian lines, but after 35 years of training, it has lowered its political aspirations.

In the economic sphere, Soviet–Korean relations are not nearly as useful a guide either to Soviet desires or to the realities of Soviet relations with east Asia. North Korea's trade with the USSR runs at less than 1 per cent of total Soviet trade although it accounts for about one-third of DPRK trade. The Soviet Union obtains certain benefits in that most of the trade is with Siberia where items like cement or cast iron can be provided by Korea at more economic rates. Given the small percentages of trade it is hardly appropriate to speak of trade surplus or deficit, but it is important to note that the balance of trade changes from year to year with no clear pattern. Thus Soviet–Korean economic relations offer few clues as to how the Soviet Union hopes to maintain economic ties with east Asia in general. Korea does not count for much in the volume of Soviet trade, nor is it a model of stability and reliability.

The military sphere of Soviet–Korean relations is much more in keeping with trends in political than in economic relations. It is striking that the peak of Soviet military involvement in Korea was in the 1940s and 1950s, and has declined ever since. Crises that involved the United States and the Soviet Union are now no longer allowed to confuse the calculations of the superpowers. The Soviet Union has withdrawn militarily from Korean affairs and this is much more in keeping with Soviet assessments of east Asia's importance.

Unfortunately from the Soviet point of view, this military withdrawal from Korea is the opposite to the general pattern of Soviet relations in the military sphere in the rest of east Asia. Indeed almost all other areas of Soviet involvement in east Asia have seen a strengthening of Soviet military power. Ground troops in Mongolia and facing China are complemented by naval forces in the Pacific facing the United States and Japan. It can be suggested that the Soviet Union would rather not have to build up these forces, but it does perceive important security problems in east Asia. Reductions in tension with the Japan–China–United States axis would be preferred, but are now seen as unlikely. Thus the Korean model of minimizing the importance of military power represents more of a Soviet objective than a description of contemporary Soviet military policy in east Asia.

In sum, the Korean model is very useful in describing at least certain aspects of Soviet policy in east Asia. The political model of relative uninvolvement reflects the reality of the Soviet position although Moscow would clearly prefer relations more along the lines of the closer Mongolian model. The military model of relative uninvolvement is the opposite case. On military matters the Soviet Union would prefer something like the Korean model of low tension, but finds itself tied down with greater commitments. Only in the economic sphere is the Korean model of little value. Soviet–Korean economic relations represent neither the objectives of Soviet policy, nor a fair representation of the present realities of Soviet economic relations with east Asia. By turning now to Soviet–Japanese relations, the economic dimension of Soviet policy might become clearer.

The Japanese model

It is clear that the Soviet Union is not, nor ever has been, pleased with the state of its relations with Japan. Therefore Soviet–Japanese relations can hardly serve as any kind of useful model for general Soviet relations in east Asia. But Moscow–Tokyo links are of interest more for what they could be than for what they are. There seems to be a great deal of potential in Soviet–Japanese relations that has not yet been exploited.

In the political sphere there have been important improvements in relations, but then that was not hard to achieve considering the low point at which they began after the Second World War. There was a time, especially in the early 1970s, when it appeared that Soviet–Japanese relations might achieve a real breakthrough, but the promise has never been fulfilled. The Soviet Union is primarily to blame for not taking sufficient initiative in breaking down the basic feature of Japanese foreign policy – the security link with the United States.

The need for a more flexible political attitude from the Soviet Union was even more acutely felt in the later 1970s when China and the Soviet Union were to a certain extent competing for Japanese favours. Moscow's failure had a great deal to do with its unwillingness to make concessions on such sensitive issues as the northern territories, and thus, if there is a nascent Japan–China–United States axis, the Soviet Union has only itself to blame. In contrast with the case of Korea, where political relations are also complex, in the Japanese case the Soviet Union has real policy options; but it refuses to exercise them.

In the economic realm, Soviet–Japanese relations are also not nearly as good as they might be, but in this case there seems to be less that the Soviet Union can do about it. The Soviet Union is clearly keen to develop Siberia with Japanese assistance and there does not appear to be any lack of will to make the minor concessions necessary to get projects off the ground.[5] The problems which prevent the fulfilment of this promising economic opportunity seem to be twofold. First, there is US pressure on Japan, as on other Western allies, to withhold sensitive equipment from the Soviet Union. US pressure for sanctions against the Soviet Union has affected the Sakhalin development project even more than it has the gas pipeline to Western Europe. Other projects in east Asian Siberia receive even less favourable treatment. But at least on this issue the Soviet Union has been able to make the persuasive point to the Japanese (and the West Europeans) that the United States is willing to fight the Soviet Union to its ally's last company, without sacrificing US firms.

But a more important obstacle to deepening economic relations is the high cost of developing east Asian Siberia because of difficult geographic conditions. To be sure, the Soviet Union will develop Siberia, whether it does it with Western assistance or not.[6] But clearly the Soviets would prefer a faster pace, and unlike the efforts to involve Western Europe in development of west Siberia, the efforts to develop east Siberia with Japan seem to be limited for more fundamental reasons that are beyond the control of the political process. This may be more frustrating, but it appears to be an unavoidable limit on Soviet–Japanese relations and Soviet economic options in east Asia. What is more, since Far Eastern issues generally take a back seat to more pressing problems, for example in Poland, Soviet–Japanese trade is occasionally sacrificed. The drastic reduction in Soviet coal deliveries to Japan in order to meet shortfalls resulting from the cutbacks in Polish supplies, only demonstrated the limits on Soviet–Japanese economic relations, and the primacy of other areas of the world for Soviet foreign policy.

The military dimension of Soviet–Japanese relations is also not nearly as good as the Soviet Union might wish, but the blame for this state of affairs lies only to a certain extent with the Soviet Union, and partially with objectively difficult defence conditions. In strategic terms the Soviet Union has limited access to the Pacific through 'choke points' which are difficult to defend. The absence of Soviet warm-water ports and the presence of the United States, Japan and China with major forces in the area does not make things easier for Moscow.

However, to a certain extent the unnecessarily high state of military confrontation between Japan and the Soviet Union is due to Moscow's own policies. It has failed to make even cosmetic concessions on the disputed islands, it has taken crude provocative military action around Japanese waters and by and large persists in its unsubtle attitudes towards Japan which are rooted in wartime hostility. It is therefore hardly surprising that Japan refuses to be enticed by the feeble Soviet attempts to reduce military confrontation.

Proposals for confidence-building measures or pledges of no first use of nuclear weapons are rejected by Japan in large measure because the Soviet Union has failed to show any real appreciation of Japanese sensitivities. Some progress can be made in the Soviet Union's military relationship with Japan, but it will require a more sophisticated Soviet political attitude in general.

In sum, if the Soviet Union is upset about the lack of progress in relations with Japan, it mostly has itself to blame. Precisely because there does seem to be something that can be done by the Soviet Union in this bilateral relationship, as opposed to many of the others under discussion, it cannot be ruled out that in the near future the Soviet Union might make a Japanese initiative. If such a move should be attempted, its main objective would be to entice Japan into developing Siberia. But unlike the political and military spheres, the obstacles in the way of economic relations seem more immovable, and less open to political initiative. If the Soviet Union has hopes in the Japanese model for economic relations, they may well be false hopes.

The Chinese model

No single aspect of Soviet policy in east Asia has been as much of a failure as Sino–Soviet relations. The transition from relative success to spectacular failure in Soviet policy in the area can be attributed primarily to Moscow's inability to manage its relations with Beijing. This is not to say that Sino–Soviet relations are unalterably frozen in hostility, but it is with this bilateral relationship that Moscow must begin if it is to make significant improvements in its Far Eastern posture.

In political terms, the most devastating strategic setback suffered by the Soviet Union since the Second World War was the 'loss of China'. No single event caused more problems in Soviet foreign policy than the transition from having China as a supportive ally to having a hostile China competing with Soviet power in the communist as well as the non-communist world. It is true that China did not become as hostile as some in Moscow feared. The United States did not manage to 'play its China card', but Chinese hostility still remained acute. What is more, unlike all the other bilateral relations already discussed, the Sino–Soviet relationship had far-reaching effects beyond the east Asian region.[7]

The roots of the Sino–Soviet split are obviously too complex to be explored here, but suffice it to say that the Soviet Union played its part in ensuring the deterioration of relations with China. Similarly Moscow is partly to blame for the continuing stalemate in Sino–Soviet relations and the damage that it does to overall Soviet policy. The recent abrogation by China of the 1950 Sino–Soviet friendship pact was more a formal seal than a major change in Sino–Soviet relations.

The obvious damage wrought by Moscow's conflict with China has not escaped decision-makers in the Kremlin. Indeed they have been making vigorous if sometimes largely cosmetic attempts in the past year to rectify the situation. Predictions on the future state of Sino–Soviet relations are difficult to make.

The Soviets have yet to make real concessions in political relations, but to a large extent it appears that change depends more on Chinese than Soviet politics. The strategic debate simmering in Beijing probably holds the key to any major improvement in Sino–Soviet relations.[8] Real concessions by the Soviet Union might well galvanize the Chinese. This is not to suggest that Sino–Soviet relations are likely to return to the 'honeymoon' of the 1950s, but a more equal balance between competition and cooperation can be expected.

The economic realm of Sino–Soviet relations has never been crucial to the Soviet Union, although in the 1950s Soviet aid was very important to the Chinese economy. This relative Chinese dependence provides the Soviet Union with a useful lever in relations with China, or at least a carrot that can be dangled as part of a package of political change. For example the renovation of Soviet-built plants from the 1950s might be achieved at a smaller cost to China than the complete overhaul needed to make use of Western equipment.

There are in fact signs that the economic dimension of Sino–Soviet relations is already leading the two states from competition towards more cooperation. Rising trade and the exchange of economic delegations in 1982 are only two of the most recent signs of change. There are however clear limits to the extent of Sino–Soviet economic cooperation from the Soviet perspective, and the Chinese model of economic relations can hardly hope to replace the Soviet dream of the Japanese model. Chinese labour in Siberia might well be useful for construction projects, but the Soviet fear of Chinese hordes sweeping across Siberia might make any such importation of labour unlikely on a large scale. In terms of oil and gas resources in Siberia and Manchuria, the Chinese and Soviets are more natural competitors than cooperators. Thus the economic dimension offers some limited hope for Soviet policy, but more as a tool of policy than for any major intrinsic value for economic development of Soviet east Asia.

In the military sphere, Sino–Soviet relations could hardly get much worse, short of war. The deployment of very impressive conventional and nuclear capability by both sides, and recent improvements in Soviet forces in the far east, make it plain that Moscow's premier military problem in east Asia is along the Sino–Soviet border.[9] Just as Beijing poses the main political problem for the Soviet Union in Asia, so China poses the main military problem. At the same time, just as there is real hope for an improvement in Sino–Soviet political relations, which Moscow can help to push along, so the Soviet Union has real options in improving the military dimension as well.

The Soviet Union has been vociferous of late in urging confidence-building measures in east Asia, and the 1982 Tashkent and Baku initiatives by President Brezhnev are only the most salient examples. But, as in the political realm, it is clear that the Soviet Union needs to take initiatives on its own to break the military stalemate, perhaps by symbolically withdrawing some troops from the frontier facing Xinjiang. Clearly there can be no return to the 1950s era of military cooperation between China and the Soviet Union, but certainly less conflict along the frontier is possible. If only by virtue of its size, place and past, China is always likely to pose some kind of threat in the eyes of Soviet planners. Thus some competition in Sino–Soviet relations seems inevitable, albeit not at the present high levels.

In sum, Sino–Soviet relations are likely to continue to be Moscow's basic problem in the Far East. This bilateral axis is unlikely to be any kind of model of cooperative relations. Nevertheless, the present enmity is not fixed in concrete and Moscow itself can take a pickaxe to the most stubborn parts. More than any other aspect of Soviet policy in Asia, the Kremlin needs to improve relations with China. If the Chinese model of relations continues to be a negative example of how to cope with east Asia, again to a large extent the Soviet Union has only itself to blame.

The United States model

Soviet–American relations are perhaps the most stable of the Soviet Union's bilateral axes in east Asia, but the stability is set at a level of significant conflict. The main reason for both the conflict and the stability is that both superpowers approach east Asia largely as great powers with far more crucial interests outside the area. Hence they regard east Asia as an area of continuing conflict, but not one in the forefront.

The political aspects of their conflict are of course rooted in broader East–West contention. But there was a time when this conflict was focused on east Asia, and primarily on Korea. At that time the struggle was relatively simple with Sino–Soviet power confronting a US-led coalition including Japan. There have of course been important changes in these relations, preeminently with the shift of China away from the Soviet pole and most recently into occasional quasi-alliance with Japan and the United States.

Such changes in political configurations have been important to the Soviet Union, but they have had little to do with changes in US policy or Soviet–US relations. Of the three states in the Japan–China–United States axis, the Soviet Union seems least concerned with the US component. To be sure the Soviet Union is concerned with US power, but Moscow appreciates that if there has been any change in the power ranged against it in east Asia, it is because China has changed its posture and not because the United States has made any important alterations to its capability. There have been no major changes in the American–Soviet confrontation in east Asia, and as can be seen in the Korean vortex, both superpowers are satisfied to 'let sleeping dogs lie' for fear of being distracted from more important conflicts elsewhere. Both superpowers are sufficiently satisfied to accept each other as superpowers, and therefore tolerate some conflict, as long as it remains stable.

In the economic realm, there is far less importance in Soviet–American relations. There are virtually no bilateral economic relations, and to the extent that the two powers are involved in economic matters, it is regarding third-party relations with the Soviet Union. For example the United States has tried to block Japanese economic deals with the Soviet Union while pouring cold water on the idea that the United States itself would become involved in Siberian development. But it would be misleading to suggest that the United States is a major impediment to Soviet–Japanese relations, for as has already been suggested the main obstacles lie in objectively difficult Siberian conditions. It is similarly incorrect to blame the United States for the limits on Sino–Soviet economic relations. Here too the problems are rooted in specific characteristics of Sino–Soviet trade, and in any case the United States and the Soviet Union have very different economic benefits to offer China. In sum, there is little of value in Soviet–American economic relations in east Asia, and nor is there likely to be much of value in the future.

The military dimension of Soviet–American relations appears to follow the pattern of political ties. There has been great stability in crisis management in superpower relations in east Asia, but both powers acknowledge that they are managing crisis and not cooperation. Both powers see their military relationship as only part of a global confrontation. In this context the United States has expressed concern with what it sees as growing Soviet naval power in east Asia.[10] Undoubtedly there have been impressive Soviet gains in the military sphere, although it is hard to see how this accretion of military power has been translated into more than just increased steel production. Certainly from the Soviet perspective, they see themselves as pursuing legitimate defensive goals in an area where there are myriad potential threats. For Moscow, the present military expansion is aimed at redressing the balance rather than seeking superiority.

It is next to impossible to sort out these counter-claims especially when each superpower is imputing worst-case intentions to its adversary. What is clear is that for paranoid military planners, east Asia provides numerous excuses for military spending. The Soviet Pacific fleet is designed to deal with threat in the complex Pacific basin area, but also through south-east Asia and the Indian Ocean. The deployments are part of global calculations rather than specific east Asian balances. What is more, while the Soviet Union is more concerned about the balance in north-east Asia, the United States has been shifting back to a primary concern with south-east Asia.[11] The military dimension of superpower relations in east Asia is therefore difficult to assess, and it is even harder to suggest that anyone has upset the balance in order to make unilateral gains.

In any case, for both superpowers the east Asian military confrontation is perhaps the least important of all potential theatres of operation. The area certainly ranks behind Europe, the Middle East and south-west

Asia among priorities for military planners. Thus, much as in their political relations, the superpowers, it seems, will carry on broadly as before, accepting continuing conflict, but within a relatively stable framework. Because the superpowers are less concerned about their east Asian confrontation and would prefer to keep matters in a low key, the pattern of Soviet–American relations in east Asia can hardly serve as a useful model for Soviet relations in the region as a whole.

Soviet policy into the 1980s

We began by seeking some pattern in Soviet policy in east Asia, and have to conclude by offering only the most generalized remarks on Soviet purposes and predicaments of power. It is relatively simple to suggest that the Soviet Union retains its four-fold objective in east Asia: (1) to ensure national security; (2) to contain Chinese power; (3) to contain US power; and (4) to contain Japanese power.

But it is equally obvious that the relative priorities attached to these policy goals do not remain constant. More importantly they are stated in such a general way because it is difficult to be more categorical about the obvious uncertainties of Soviet power in east Asia. No clear-cut answer is possible for those seeking to know whether the Soviet Union is more threatening than threatened, or more prudent than paranoid in its policy. In the final analysis the Soviets seem to engage in all these actions, often at the same time and in different areas. Academic models of inter-state behaviour may make for neat concluding chapters, but they do not begin to come to grips with the complex reality in east Asia.

What is perhaps more useful is to suggest the 'models' of relations that the Soviet Union might hope to establish in east Asia, and where there is scope for real change. In the political realm, the model of Soviet–Korean relations, wherein the Soviet Union reluctantly accepts the predicaments of power, seems to be the most likely future. While Moscow could clearly prefer the Mongolian model of docility, it has come to accept the unreality of such a prospect. In this political realm there are however three states, Japan, China and the United States, whose relations with the Soviet Union are far from even the relatively controlled Korean model of conflict. To alter the degree of hostility with these three powers is to a certain extent within the power of the Soviet Union. Concessions, especially to China and Japan, would seem to be a priority for Soviet policy, but there can also be little optimism that Moscow will take up the challenge. The failures of policy are, to an important extent, ones of the Soviet Union's own making.

In economic relations, the model relationship has yet to be established. The Soviet–Japanese axis held great promise at one point, but the dream has faded in recent years. The Soviet Union has powerful hopes of developing east Asian Siberia, and neither Mongolia's, nor

Korea's, nor even now China's, economic relations with the Soviet Union offer a chance of fulfilling these dreams. Only Japan, and to a much more minor extent the United States, can help in the economic realm, and there can be little confidence in Moscow that such help will be forthcoming in the near future.

In the military realm, as in the political realm, the model of Soviet Korean relations seems the most likely realistic objective of Soviet policy. Once again the Soviet Union would prefer the peaceful and pro-Soviet Mongolian model, but it seems to have accepted that the region's complexity will not permit such utopian solutions. Once again as in the political realm, the main challenges and prospects for change in Soviet military policy lie in the hope of modifying the conflict with China, Japan and the United States. There seems to be little that can be done about the confrontation with US power as that is a function of global superpower rivalry which has more complex sources and patterns. Soviet–Japanese military confrontation can be eased somewhat, but as in the political realm, the key seems to lie in Soviet concessions, especially on the northern islands. Most crucially, the Soviet Union needs a reduction of tension along the Sino–Soviet frontier. Some change is possible, but China's insistence that Moscow take the first concrete step to build confidence seems valid. A dramatic and real step by Moscow, for example by limited troop withdrawals in Mongolia, would certainly show more policy innovation than has lately been evident from the Soviet Union.

Soviet policy in east Asia into the 1980s does hold some prospect for change. But if Moscow would truly like to control 'the forces of history', it needs to take its destiny far more into its own hands. Concrete actions in political and military relations, especially with Japan and China, are needed. Previous Soviet policy in east Asia does not suggest such boldness is likely, but it is possible. Whatever the specific action by the Soviet Union, the natural complexity of east Asian international relations is likely to ensure that opportunities for change will always remain.

Notes
[1] Allen Whiting, *Siberian Development and East Asia* (Stanford, Calif., Stanford University Press, 1981).
[2] Robert Rupen, *How Mongolia Is Really Ruled* (Stanford, Calif., Hoover Institution Press, 1979).
[3] Xinhua domestic service in Chinese, 5 April 1982, in Foreign Broadcast Information Service (FBIS) Chi-82-065-D1.
[4] R. Rupen, *How Mongolia Is Really Ruled*; also Charles Bawden, *The Modern History of Mongolia* (New York, Praeger, 1968).

[5]   V. Alexandrov, 'Siberia and the Soviet far east in Soviet–Japanese economic relations', *Far Eastern Affairs* (Moscow), no. 2 (1982).

[6]   A. Whiting, *Siberian Development*.

[7]   Gerald Segal (ed.), *The China Factor* (London, Croom Helm, 1982).

[8]   Gerald Segal, 'China's security debate', *Survival*, vol. 24, no. 2 (March–April 1982).

[9]   Paul Dibb, 'Soviet capabilities, interests and strategies in east Asia in the 1980's', *Survival*, vol. 24, no. 4 (July–August 1982); and John Erickson, 'The Soviet strategic emplacement in Asia', *Asian Affairs*, February 1981.

[10]   Robert Scalapino, 'The U.S. and east Asia: views and policies in a changing era', *Survival*, vol. 24, no. 4 (July–August 1982).

[11]   *International Herald Tribune*, 8 June 1982.

Index

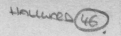